D1628019

ARNOLD WESKER (F.R.S.L., Litt.D.), born in Stepney in 1932, was taught at Upton House School in Hackney. His education came mainly from reading books and listening to BBC Radio. From 1948 to 1958 he pursued many trades from furniture maker to pastry cook. His career as a playwright began when Lindsay Anderson, who had read *The Kitchen* and *Chicken Soup with Barley*, brought Wesker to the attention of George Devine at the Royal Court Theatre; Devine, uncertain about *Chicken Soup with Barley*, sent it to the Belgrade Theatre in Coventry, where it was first produced in 1958 under the direction of John Dexter. A year later, having been turned down by the Royal Court, *Roots* was directed by Dexter, again at the Belgrade, Coventry, and in the following months he directed *The Kitchen* at the Court for two Sunday night experimental performances 'without decor'. Later in 1959 *I'm Talking about Jerusalem* was added to make up *The Wesker Trilogy*, which created an enormous impact when produced in its entirety at the Royal Court in 1960 and again at the Shaw Theatre in 1978. In 1979 the National Film Development Board commissioned a film script of the three plays, which, because Wesker made many cuts and additions, is a new work – *The Trilogy* twenty years on! Over 350,000 copies of the Penguin edition have been sold, and the hardback is in its fifth printing.

His other plays are *Chips with Everything* (1962, voted 'Play of the Year'), *Their Very Own and Golden City* (1965, winner of the Italian Premio Marzotto Drama Award in 1964), *The Four Seasons* (1965), *The Friends* (1970), *The Old Ones* (1972), *The Journalists* (1972), *The Wedding Feast* (1974), *Shylock* (1975, previously entitled *The Merchant*), *Love Letters on Blue Paper* (1977), *One More Ride on the Merry Go Round* (1978), *Caritas* (1980), *Annie Wobbler* (1981), *Four Portraits – of Mothers* (1982), *Yardsale* (1984), *Whatever Happened to Betty Lemon?* (1986), *The Mistress* (1988); these last five form the cycle of *One-Woman Plays*; *Bluey* (1984, European Radio Commission), *Sullied Hand* (1985), *When God Wanted a Son* (1986), *Badenheim 1939* (1987), *Lady Othello* (1987), *Beorhtel's Hill* (1988, community play commissioned for the 40th anniversary of Basildon).

In addition to plays for the stage Arnold Wesker has written television and film scripts, poems, short stories and numerous essays and lectures. He has published two collections of essays, *Fears of Fragmentation* (1970) and *Distinctions* (1985), and three volumes of stories, *Six Sundays in January* (1971), *Love Letters on Blue Paper* (1974) and *Said the Old Man to the Young Man* (1978). In 1974 he wrote the text for a book of primitive paintings of the East End by John Allin, *Say Goodbye You May Never See Them Again*. In 1977, after a brief stay in the offices of *The Sunday Times* to gather material for *The Journalists*, he published an account of his visit called *Journey into Journalism*. In 1978 came *Fatlips*, his only book for young people. Penguin have published six volumes of his plays and a collection of short stories under the title *Love Letters on Blue Paper*.

From 1961 to 1970 Arnold Wesker was artistic director of Centre 42, a cultural movement for popularizing the arts primarily through trade-union support and participation. From 1981 to 1983 he was President of the International Playwrights' Committee. He is a grandfather and lives with his wife and one of his three children in North London.

ARNOLD WESKER

ONE-WOMAN PLAYS

Yardsale
Whatever Happened to Betty Lemon?
Four Portraits – of Mothers
The Mistress
Annie Wobbler

VOLUME 5

PENGUIN BOOKS

PENGUIN BOOKS

Published by the Penguin Group
27 Wrights Lane, London W8 5TZ, England
Viking Penguin Inc., 40 West 23rd Street, New York, New York 10010, USA
Penguin Books Australia Ltd, Ringwood, Victoria, Australia
Penguin Books Canada Ltd, 2801 John Street, Markham, Ontario, Canada L3R 1B4
Penguin Books (NZ) Ltd, 182–190 Wairau Road, Auckland 10, New Zealand

Penguin Books Ltd, Registered Offices: Harmondsworth, Middlesex, England

Yardsale first published in *Plays International* April 1987

Whatever Happened to Betty Lemon? first published in German in *Englisch-Amerikanische Studien*, Munich 1986
First published in English in *Plays International* April 1987

Four Portraits – of Mothers first published in *Stand* Winter 1987–8

The Mistress first published by Penguin Books 1989

Annie Wobbler first published in Italian in the programme of Teatro Festival Parma April 1986
First published in English in *Words International* December 1987 and January 1988

This collection first published 1989
1 3 5 7 9 10 8 6 4 2

All rights whatsoever are reserved and application for performance, etc., should be made in writing
to Ian Amos, Duncan Heath Associates, 162 Wardour Street, London W1V 4AT

Made and printed in Great Britain by
Cox and Wyman Ltd, Reading, Berks.
Filmset in 10/12 Linotron Goudy by
Rowland Phototypesetting Ltd, Bury St Edmunds, Suffolk

CONTENTS

Introduction
7

Yardsale
9

Whatever Happened to Betty Lemon?
23

Four Portraits – of Mothers
37

The Mistress
55

Annie Wobbler
79

INTRODUCTION

These plays for one actress were written over a period of five years.

Tucked within those years I wrote four full-length plays for between three and fifty characters, a 90-minute play for radio for seventeen characters, a libretto for an opera of my play *Caritas*, two one-act plays for schools with casts of seven plus, a TV adaptation of Arthur Koestler's novel *Thieves in the Night* for a cast of dozens upon dozens, and at the time of writing this introduction I am writing *a community play* for a cast of hundreds!

I feel the need to establish this background to the one-woman plays because some people imagine that one-woman plays are *all* I've written in five years.

Not that I am apologizing for writing this cycle of plays for one actress. In no way do I consider them slight pieces. There is a view of the one-person play that dismisses them as of little consequence because they are 'for only one actor'. Why? We do not dismiss the great works for solo instrument simply because they are 'for only one instrument'. Is it an inconsequential part of his talent that has gone into the composition of the magnificent Beethoven sonatas for piano – the 'Moonlight', the 'Pathétique', the 'Appassionata'?

Similarly the best of whatever is my talent and intelligence has gone into these plays for one woman.

I also persist in using the word 'play' and not 'monologue' to describe them. I understand a mono-logue to be one person merely speaking *and not engaged in any action*. A monologue for one actor suggests a person thinking out loud and addressing no one else; a play for one actor suggests a person responding to a situation or involved in an action and engaged in an exchange of conflict.

With those definitions in mind none of these plays can be described as monologues. In each one there is either 'someone else' being addressed – whether it is Annie Wobbler talking to 'madam and God' offstage, or Annabella talking to imaginary journalists, or Betty

7

Lemon talking to her noose; or there is an activity, an action taking place, such as Stephanie cooking and making trips out to overcome her depression; such as Samantha cutting out the pattern of one of her dresses. Mostly both things are happening – someone else is addressed while an action is taking place.

So, this is a volume of plays not monologues, and as such they have most of the qualities one expects from a play – complex structure, interaction between people (even if only the different people within the one person), cause and effect, development and/or evolvement, rhythm, dramatic dialogue, metaphor and resonance.

They may not be plays that succeed in what they set out to achieve; that is another matter, they are in the hands of their public and posterity. I write this introduction simply to ask that they be considered for what they are, not dismissed for what they are not.

Finally, the order of the plays follows a chronology more of spirit than time.

ARNOLD WESKER
Hay-on-Wye, 13 July 1988

YARDSALE

Yardsale was first broadcast by BBC Radio 3 on 6 October 1984 with Sheila Steafel, produced by Margaret Windham. It had its stage premiere on 12 August 1985 at the Edinburgh Festival with Jeannie Fisher, directed by Eric Standige. Its first London performance was in a double-bill with *Whatever Happened to Betty Lemon?* on 17 February 1987 at the Lyric Theatre Studio, Hammersmith, with Brenda Bruce, directed by the author and designed by Jackie Pilfold.

Scene i: The homecoming

Brooklyn, New York State. A suburban house. Front door closing. STEPHANIE, *a primary schoolteacher around forty-eight, returns home, takes off her coat, boots . . . mimed. Prepares a meal . . . mimed. The tick of a clock divides the parts.*

STEPHANIE

I'm late, I'm late, don't tell me – I'm late! But there are reasons. Not because I kept any of my children behind in class. Not because I was kept talking by one of those drive-you-crazy-my-child's-genius-is-being-neglected mothers. Not because the bus was held up by all this snow which made my boots wet and reminds me I've got to buy a new pair which it so happens I saw on sale in that store which seems to have a non-stop-all-the-year-round sale so you wonder where they get their stock from. Not because of any *one* of those things but because of *all* of them put together plus I saw this gorgeous pullover for you which I had to buy and they didn't have your size but they told me they could get it sent over from another of their stores which wouldn't take a minute they said but it took thirty so I'm five minutes later than usual but here it is and here I am, your one-and-only Stephanie and soon we can eat. (*Sung as in 'Jeal-ous-y'*) Steph–an–ie!

Sheldon? Don't you delay now. We promised we'd go hear Lord What's-his-name from England lecture on who has stolen what art treasures from whom and should they be returned. So move your butt and join me in the kitchen for a rousing chorus of 'Summertime' and we'll chop mushrooms together. Remember:

Procrastination is the thief of time;

Year after year it steals till all are fled

And to the mercies of a moment leaves

The vast concerns of an eternal scene.

Lord What's-his-name may not be a vast concern but let's not leave ourselves to the mercies of a moment.

Sheldon? Sheldon? Only *five* minutes late. Is he upstairs in the bathroom and I uttered all that to the air? (*Looks high and low.*) Sheldon? Are you sulking somewhere because I'm five minutes late? You can't call 'five minutes' five minutes late! Sheldon, are you anywhere in the house? (*Beat.*) Has he kept some of his kids behind in class?

(*Begins to prepare meal. Mimes slicing and slapping and frying.*)

Poor Sheldon. It's harder work teaching teenagers than primary schoolkids. I'm luckier than him. Wrong! Than he is.

From five years old to seven you're embarrassed, from seven to nine you're grateful, from nine to eleven you're beginning to be confident – after that everything collapses and you've got to start all over again: confidence-building, ego-tripping, sexual-flaunting, parent-confronting, teacher-challenging, world-mocking, everything boiling and troubling and nuclear-exploding. Right, Sheldon? Right, Stephanie!

Sheldon, are you sure you're not somewhere in the house? I know your tricks, you let me talk to myself and that way imagine you're hearing what I really think but never tell you. I'm not one of your devious-imagining-they're-subtle women, you know, or one of your hesitant-imagining-they're-thoughtful women, or one of your obscure-imagining-they're-profound women. I tell you everything and say what I mean which is not always sensible, you're right, but there you are, I am who I am what I am that I am so you can listen to me talking to myself all the time and you won't find out more than you already know about me. Sheldon?

I've always been luckier than him. Than he is. To begin with I've got him and he's only got me. (*Beat.*) Now then, Stephie, don't let your feminist friends hear you talk that way, putting yourself down. (*Singing*) Steph–an–ie! So what if your breasts droop and you've got piles? Teachers sit down they get piles! Poets and long-distance truck-drivers also get piles. And if Sheldon had had three children his breasts would also droop. (*Beat.*) More than they do! (*Laughs.*) Naughty. You should be naughty more often. Right, Sheldon? Right, Stephanie! (*Singing*) Steph–an–ie!

There! That's the steaks slapped and peppered, the potatoes scrubbed and baking, the mushrooms chopped and frying, the tomatoes grilling . . .

(*Singing*) . . . an' the livin' is easy.

Fish are jumpin' and the cotton is high.

Oh your daddy's rich and your ma is good lookin'.

Hush, little baby, don't you cry.

(*Beat.*) Think I'll put on some music, perhaps a candle, freshen my make-up a little, drooping breasts or no drooping breasts. (*Singing*) Steph–an–ie!

12

(Dims lights. Lights a candle. Puts on a cassette. Second movement of Barber Violin Concerto. Goes into bedroom. Lights fade.)

Scene ii: The discovery

Lights up. STEPHANIE *is holding a letter.*

STEPHANIE

Oh no, Sheldon. Not me. Please not to me. Please, please not to this old friend. Not after twenty-five years and three children, and all that history, Sheldon. Twenty-five years and three children is history, rich and private and all ours. Ours! Ours and yours and mine and theirs and all rich and private and not for sharing. With anyone. No one. Oh, please God, don't let it be happening to me. Please, oh please.

(She weeps. Slowly controls herself.)

(Reading) 'My dear Stephie.' My dear Stephie? His? He's leaving and claiming me at the same time. Strange man. 'My dear Stephie. I must go. We care about one another but there is no more we have to give one another. Not you to me, not me to you. We say nothing at mealtimes, we feel nothing at bedtimes, we know everything and too much and nothing is a surprise. Curiosity gone, nerve-ends dead, mechanical. We are boring. I need to be able to surprise someone.'

I'm surprised, Sheldon, am I surprised! Don't go, look! I'm very surprised. *(Beat.)* I'm mortified. *(Beat.)* I'm destroyed.

(Music fades. Lights dim.)

Scene iii: The depression

She is curled up in a bed or divan. Foetal position.

STEPHANIE

I will lie here in this bed and never get up. They can do without me in school. The children don't need me. For weeks I've done nothing but yell at them, anyway. I will lie here in this bed and invent agonies for her.

What did I do wrong? Husband thief!

I will lie here in this bed and invent agonies fit for a husband thief!

Was my skin clammy? Was my voice droning? *Were* my thoughts boring?

I would like to pull out her nails. No. Better. I would like to tie *her* up to watch while I pull out *his* nails. No. Better. I would like to tie them both up while I mark her and castrate him and then pull out their nails. First one from him then one from her then one from him then one from her. She loves him, she loves him not, she loves him, she loves him not, she loves him. (*Beat.*) She loves him. (*Beat.*) Oh Christ, does she love him?

What, what did I do wrong?

I will lie here in this bed and drown. Who needs a teacher with such violence in her? (*Beat.*) They say your whole life flashes by you when you drown. I'm drowning and I want my whole life to flash by me to see where I went wrong.

Stephanie! Why should you think *you* went wrong? (*Singing*) Steph–an–ie! I would like to see her run over by a car. I would like to see her struck blind. I would like to take shit and throw it on her. I will lie here in this bed and imagine these things.

Did my breath smell? Did I talk nonsense? Did I lack style?

I've been a good woman, Sheldon. Faithful, patient, a companion, a friend, and I laid on my back more times than I cared to for you, you know that? There! More times than I cared to. Surprises? You want surprises? There's a surprise for you. I opened my legs and thought about cooking the next day's meal while you heaved and puffed and made all those absurd shrieks you informed me was passion. 'Passion,' you yelled at me. 'Be passionate! Moan.' I'm moaning, Sheldon. Listen how I'm moaning now. Oh God, how I moan. I will lie here in this bed and never get up and I will moan the rest of my days.

Was I too loud, too intense, too dry? Did something in me stop too long ago?

You don't know what you've done. You can't know or you wouldn't have done it. Did you think? You never think. A woman past her best, her three children grown up, disappeared into their own lives. I've invested in you my youth, my womanhood, the secrets of my body, my fund of love, friendship, wisdom and patience, and my investments should be showing a return, damn it! I should be plucking the profits by now!

But you have taken them. Run off with them. Snatched them from under my nose to share with someone else. Thief, Sheldon! Miserable bastard thief! Criminal thief! Stop, thief! Stop, stop, thief! Stop, murderer!

I will lie here in my bed and never get up and be in darkness, and I will moan and see no one. Ever again.

Scene iv: The phone call

STEPHANIE *is speaking to a friend on the phone.*

STEPHANIE

Maxie? Maxie, have you got a second? Well, not a second, a couple of days, actually. Yes I received the carrot cake and the chicken breasts and the saucepan full of chilli con carne – thank you but you're cooking for armies! I'm a single woman, remember? Nevertheless, I thank you, thank you, all of you. You worry, you nag, but now don't interrupt me, I've got to talk.

I've been thinking. Thinking and remembering and remembering and thinking and I've made discoveries and come to conclusions. I'm a fool! Worse, I'm a dishonest fool! I'm a fool because I married a man I never really loved; and I'm a dishonest fool because I pretended I loved him.

I never loved him! I didn't even like him. I thought I loved him because he said he loved me and – and this is the trap into which, oh boy!, didn't I fall – he was the first man ever to say it. 'I love you!' Imagine! I was twenty-four and beginning to think I was a leper or my breath was permanently putrefied, and along comes this man, this young god built on fresh eggs, orange juice, his mother's chopped liver, and the playing fields of Brooklyn High, with green eyes and curly hair and a cherubic smile from Botticelli which you want to eat and says, 'I love you!' To me! Who could resist? He had to be an extraordinary human being to love me, and who was I not to be in love with an extraordinary human being?

But think about him. I mean, when I think about him, I mean – oh good God and little fishes – did he have a mind? I mean, a mind? You know what I mean by a mind, don't you? That lovely thing which takes from here and connects with there and interprets this and illuminates that. Him? Ponderous like a hedgehog. Not one prick but many! Every day he was run over by a world he never comprehended.

And what conversation! He floated the debris of other people's battles. His thoughts used to go on for so long his words would forget where they began. Dialogue like driftwood – sodden and cut off. He was a thief! What could you expect? He stole my youth and other people's arguments. A thief!

And was he witty? Was he ever! *She* was witty. I've got to give the husband thief that. Smart, witty, rich and healthy. So healthy it made you sick to look at her, you know the type I mean? But him? Jokes fell off him like shoes fall off tired old men. He told stories back to front at the wrong time to the wrong people and for the wrong reasons. He should never have tried to amuse. It's a talent. He didn't have the talent. I used to get embarrassed the way friends laughed from embarrassment. But could he see it? Never! I never knew a man so insensitive to what was happening around him. And his puns? Did you ever know a grown person so relentlessly persist in what must be one of *the* most boring literary exercises ever conceived? It was an illness with him. A mental twitch. Couldn't control himself. Some men can't control their gas, he couldn't control his urge to pun. And how he preened himself when he'd let it out. Did you notice? That slow grin and that self-satisfied glance around the company for approval? In one man there resided (*giggles*) the farter, the pun and the holy boast! Jokes! What am I making jokes for? I want to make murder!

And you should have seen him in bed. Or rather you shouldn't have seen him in bed. I'm sorry I ever saw him in bed. 'Tonight's the night,' he'd announce. Subtly. 'Faw what, honey?' I used to put on a shy, Southern drawl and pretend I didn't know what he was on about. 'What night's this, sugar plum? You all surely don't mean – oh my, Sheldon, there's no stopping you I do declare.' And then he'd leap on to the bed in his altogether and start jumping up and down so's his shlong and spheroids flip-flapped about his thighs and I'd have to join him and bounce alongside of him so's my titties went flip-flap too and we made such a right old slap-smacking sound that I'm certain all the neighbours could hear. Sensuality, Maxie? He had the sensuality of a rhino stuck in mud, of a crocodile with false teeth, of a baboon full of fleas, a crab, a snail, a hyena, a pterodactyl! And all because he said he loved me.

What am I gonna do? What am I gonna do, what? Tell me what? What, what, what?

VISITS TO HELP FORGET

Scene v: To the art gallery

She's in the Whitney Museum of American art.

STEPHANIE

Go out, said my friends, visit places, out and about. Behave like the still-living, the still-curious, the still-mentally-alert-and-lively Stephanie we all knew and loved. (*Singing*) Steph–an–ie! So! I'm out and about! But what am I out about? I'm out but what am I about? I should about turn and get out of this gallery, that's what I should do, not stay here and look at this painter Hopper who I once loved because – I used to explain to our circle with earnest admiration – he exemplified the desperation and loneliness of men and women in a big city. Desperation! Loneliness! What am I looking at such paintings for? I'm not lonely and desperate enough? Go out, said my friends, visit places. But every place I go reminds me of him, of us, of our young years together. Stolen from me. Poisoned for me. Art galleries, museums, theatres, parks, bookshops, restaurants . . .

Scene vi: To the restaurant

She's in Serendipity, a restaurant famous in New York for its huge desserts.

STEPHANIE

. . . restaurants, take-aways, bars, flea markets, even here, Serendipity's, where we'd each order an over-sized knickerbocker glory or hot-fudge sundae, and laugh and laugh and laugh. Poisoned!

What am I doing here? Mad-brained Stephanie! Don't you know that everywhere will be a sentimental journey? Everything will make you want to cry? I can't listen to music any more, I can't read poetry any more. I look at children, I cry. If it rains, I cry. The sun shines, I still cry. Massacres! Famine! Lovers holding hands! Cry, cry, cry! I've become a weepy!

17

Go out, said my friends, stay living. So I'm out and living and among crowds and I've never felt so lonely in all my life.

And do I need such a large dessert? Did I ever need such a large dessert? For such large desserts I've got my just deserts – fat and abandoned and growing fatter by the hour. This ice-cream, it's like my marriage was – too big, too cold, and melting.

I hope he melts for her too, her the husband thief. Smart, witty, rich, and ridiculously healthy – but a husband thief no matter which way you look at it, and I'm looking at it all ways, all the time non-stop, scrutinizing every detail of him, of me, of the past, to see what went wrong.

Go out, said my friends. Go jogging, go swimming, change your hairstyle, buy clothes, sell your house, get yourself massaged . . .

Scene vii: To the bookshop

She's in Barnes and Noble.

STEPHANIE

A bookshop! What am I doing in a bookshop? I've got wall-to-wall books I haven't read, that I can't read, that I've no appetite to read, and here I am contemplating buying more when what I have didn't help. What would I do with more knowledge?

Stupid question! And you a teacher. You're full of stupid questions. Your brain's going to pieces. You're a joy to no one.

Anthologies of Shakespeare, anthologies of poetry. Reprints, art prints, paintings and sculptures, cartoons and cookery. Books of photographs, of foreign places. Visit foreign places, said my friends. Look at them! Who conceived so many editions? Who were they aimed at? Who's going to buy them for Christ's sake?

There is something about abundance makes you feel a theft here and there wouldn't be missed. (*Beat.*) What am I saying? Me! A remainder among remainders.

Scene viii: Yardsale

Sunday morning church bells. STEPHANIE *has just arrived. The first one there. No owner around. She begins by waiting outside.*

STEPHANIE

Go out, said my friends. Great! What does the notice say? (*Reading*) 'Yardsale of the century takes place here. Sunday, 18 September 1986. Nine thirty sharp.' It is Sunday, September 18, 1986, and it's nine forty-five sharp!

Sharp? Why should time be sharp? 'On the dot' I understand. But 'sharp'? On the sharp dot, maybe. Ah! Of course! Be here on the sharp dot of nine thirty. Only they dropped the 'dot'. (*Beat.*) And it's no longer nine thirty. It's (*looks at watch*) nine forty-six and forty-five seconds. (*Pause.*) Nine forty-six and fifty seconds. (*Pause.*) Nine forty-six and fifty-five seconds. (*Pause.*) Nine forty-seven! Sharp!

Why do I talk about time all the time? And why am I on time all the time? Was I too pedantic? Is *that* what was wrong?

(*She 'enters' the yard, talks as she picks up and regards objects.*)
And why do I come nosing around sales looking, looking, as though I was a newly-wed with a new home to set up, always the first one here, even before the owner of the yard where the yardsale of the century is about to take place, is up? (*Pause.*) Nine forty-eight!

And that's how life goes and still no one's here to say hello, how are you, welcome to our yardsale of the century, here's a tired old coat-hanger, a three-legged chair, an old-fashioned mirror, an old-fashioned typewriter, an old-fashioned waltz.

(*She hums waltz and waltzes a little. Stops. Pauses.*)
Nine forty-nine! (*Calling*) Hey, mister, I could steal things. (*Beat.*) Trusting souls!

And what do we have here? A photo album. What kind of people throw away their relatives? In fact, come to think of it, what kind of people throw away their homes? You come to a sale like this and the question must be asked: why is all this discarded? Why should I want what someone else has discarded? What makes me think I could grow to love what someone else has squeezed all the love from? You come to a sale like this, the question has got to be asked.

Why do I ask? I know. You get tired of things. Even lovely things. I know. I had a husband got tired of me. In fact the person I knew was best at these yardsales of the century, who knew which ones to come to and which to avoid, and where to look first, and what was a real bargain, and who was there sharp on the dot, on the sharp dot, on the dot – sharp! – was the woman who talked my husband into thinking he was tired of me.

But we won't talk about her. Even though she's smart, witty, rich and healthy, we will not talk about her.

And what do we have here? A box full of postcards? I don't understand it. People write to you – it means something! A hello-how-are-you! Me, I hang on to 'hellos'. When your husband's gone after twenty-five years, three children, drooping breasts, dreams of murder, loss of faith, loss of confidence, loss of friends, a hysterectomy and a year of piles – you need all the 'hellos' you can get. Miss Husband Thief!

I know, I know. People collect cards: sea views, mountains, old towns, old beauties, old stamps, old hellos.

Miss Husband Thief! Miss Long Beak, Miss Hawk's Eyes, Miss Sensitive Schnozzle. From yardsales like this she furnished *his* new home. *Their* new home. 'Look at this!' she'd say. 'Gold! And guess what I paid for it – two dollars!' Everything only ever cost her two dollars. And I'd get excited. Can you imagine? She was planning my husband's new home and I was getting excited. There's a fool for you? Would you believe a woman who should know better because she's a woman could be such a trusting fool? But we won't talk about her even though she's smart, witty, rich and healthy so it makes you sick.

It's a funny thing, a yardsale. You come to buy the things you didn't know you needed.

Baby carriage, cradle, trunks, cushions, curtains, shoes, candle-sticks, ornaments, tools, linen, cardboard boxes full of – of – everything!

Why are they getting rid of all these items? Has someone died? The children gone? Why aren't the children inheriting?

Didn't they ever love these things?

On the other hand – it can be exciting. A box full of everything is exciting. You got to admit, in a box full of everythings you could find anythings. Beads, dolls, bricks, old thimbles, paperweights, pens. People actually collect old fountain pens. I never knew. She told me. Miss Useless Information.

She'd come back with these things and talk about them, where she was going to put them, how she was going to repair them, all about their period. She was clever. You've got to hand it to her, she knew things. I used to think how fortunate we were to have such a scintillating friend. 'Bright Eyes' I called her. I used to be proud we knew her. Boasted to our friends.

'You must meet our Miss Bright Eyes!' Miss Bright Eyes, Miss Knowledgeable, Miss Widely Read, Miss Much Travelled, Miss Stunning Taste, Miss Body Beautiful, Miss God Damned Healthy Slimy Husband Thief! I want to skin her alive and make her watch while I have handbags, gloves, and slippers-to-walk-on-high-fashioned from her slimy skin!

But we will not talk about her.

The old pens I've thrown out! And the baby carriages, cradles, trunks, cushions, curtains – husbands!

Nine fifty-five!

What am I doing here? Pouncing on other people's used objects. I need new objects to hang new memories, my memories. What do I need other people's old loves for? Mrs Garbage Items!

(*Calling*) Hey, mister! Come, already! A half-hour I've been here.

(*Weeping*) I could steal things.

   (*Lights fade.*)

WHATEVER HAPPENED TO
BETTY LEMON?

Whatever Happened to Betty Lemon? was first performed on 12 November 1986 at the Théâtre du Rond-Point, Paris, with Judit Magre, directed by Jean-Michel Ribes. Its first London performance was in a double-bill with *Yardsale* on 17 February 1987 at the Lyric Theatre Studio, Hammersmith, with Brenda Bruce, directed by the author and designed by Jackie Pilfold.

An Edwardian mansion flat.

Four areas in four corners: the front door, the study, the lounge, the kitchen. In the centre sits an electric wheelchair.

Off-centre hangs a rope looking like a noose, without the hangman's knot.

A whirring clock strikes seven. A lavatory flushes.

BETTY LEMON, *an old woman crippled by everything old age brings. Eccentric. She hobbles in with the aid of a walking frame. Surveys her flat. Another day is beginning. Gloom. She looks at the noose. It is her daily companion with whom she converses. From it she draws strength, determination, as though she has deliberately erected a confrontation with the ultimate in order to be challenged.*

A glance at the noose gives her resolve to face the day's battles with obstacles she's determined to overcome.

First to the front door to draw out a newspaper. A letter drops with it. She cannot be bothered to bend and pick it up. Now to the study to deposit the paper and collect a dirty cup and saucer. She cannot negotiate the frame and the crockery. She abandons frame, reaches for a walking stick, hobbles to kitchen to deposit cup and saucer.

Now to the lounge to switch on the television. She cannot bear the early-morning cheerfulness. Turns it off. Hobbles back to the front door to retrieve letter. It has all been too exhausting. She struggles to the wheelchair into which she collapses.

BETTY

I didn't fucking plan it this way.

(*Reading*) 'Dear Lady Lemon . . .' (*Savouring it*) Lady Lemon. He promised he'd become a knight before he died. And he did. Then he died. Honoured and penniless. Though he spent his seed more than his pennies. Philandering bastard! Sir James Lemon! Socialist MP for Birmingham North. Knighted for services rendered to the nation. (*Beat.*) For services rendered at night to the fucking nation, more like!

(*Reading*) 'Dear Lady Lemon . . .'

They call me 'madam' when I attend functions. 'Ma'am' sometimes. 'Honoured Ma'am . . .' 'This plaque is dedicated, Ma'am . . .' 'We would like you to meet, Ma'am . . .' Me. Betty Lemon née Rivkind from Dalston Junction. If only they'd known my father. 'Rubbish!' he said. 'They all talk rubbish!'

(*Reading*) 'Dear Lady Lemon . . .'

Madam Betty Lemon. Madam Betty Bitter Lemon. Madam Letty Batty Melon. Madam Batty Smelly Salmon. Smelly Betty Satin Button. Keep your hat on. Steel your baton. Bolt your belly button, Betty. Oh belt up, Lady Lemon. (*Beat.*) You go daft when no one's around.

(*Reading*) 'Dear Lady Lemon . . .'

You need someone around to stop you going daft. (*Beat.*) You wouldn't think I'd once been brainy. 'Watch out for brainy Betty Lemon,' they'd say. I was what they called an intellectual.

(*To the noose*) Difficult to be an intellectual when no one's around to challenge you.

(*Reading*) 'Dear Lady Lemon. It is with great pleasure that I inform you you have been chosen Handicapped Woman of the Year . . .'

(*Incredulity. A thought so bizarre she can hardly accommodate it.*)

Handi-what of the year? Me? They telling me there's no one more handicapped in the entire fucking universe than me? And they're crowning me for it! What glorious son of man conceived such blushing laurels, such awesome accolades, such canonization? (*Thinks about it.*) Champion Cripple, three cheers! Happy Hobbler of the Year, hurrah! The Season's Paraplegic Princess, pah pom!

(*She's amused herself. Giggles. Stops abruptly.*)

(*Reading*) 'As you may know, the Society for the Elderly Handicapped holds an annual dinner at which the Handicapped Woman of the Year and the Handicapped Man of the Year each address us for half an hour on how they overcame their handicaps . . .'

Who says I over-fucking-came them?

(*She rehearses her address. Not to the audience.*)

'My Lords, Ladies and Gentlemen, sound or unsound, firm or infirm, those glowing with health or those ugly with pain. I had an uncle – yes, even old women may once have had uncles – I had an uncle who, recovering from his third heart operation declared to me: "You think the world is divided into social classes, don't you? As a socialist," he said, "you think the big divide in life is between those who have and those who have not. Well, let me tell you you are wrong," he said. "The world is divided into those who have health and those who do not have health. *That's* the only division that counts." Was he right or was he wrong, my Lords, Ladies and

Gentlemen? (*Waits.*) Come on, let's hear from you. Was he right or was he bloody wrong? (*Waits.*) Right! He was bloody right!'

(*Returns to letter.*)

(*Reading*) 'We can offer you a fee . . .'

How very kind.

Now then, Betty Lemon. No bitterness. Remember you're a lai-dy, and though your famous, revered, socially responsible, ever-smiling, much-loved husband who talked rubbish all his life is dead they've not forgotten his wife, the loud-mouthed cow, the sardonic shadow, the caustic, unappreciative bitch at his side, Handicapped Woman of the Year! Handi-fucking-capped-woman-of-the-year-Betty-Lemon-honoured-and-remembered! You should feel proud. Chosen. One of the chosen. (*Beat.*) And look what happened to them!

'My Lords, Ladies and Gentlemen. I had an aunt – yes, even old women may once have had aunts – I had an aunt who while burning at the stake – well, not literally but you know what I mean – said: "Betty," she said, "never be chosen, never stand out in a crowd. If you have ideas, keep them to yourself; if you have opinions, suppress them. Never argue with those in charge, those in authority, those with power. Dress soberly, live modestly, don't shout or become emotional or fall in love, if you have to fall in love try to do it without passion. The majority", she said, "are mediocre and filled with such venomous hatred they'll slice you into bloody little bloody bits of little bloody pieces. Betty Lemon," she said, "keep your nose clean and never be chosen."'

(*Returns to letter.*)

(*Reading*) '. . . and you will be collected and delivered home to your door . . .'

(*Crying out to the noose*) What about those handicapped by their impoverished imaginations, eh? What about a dinner for *them*? Aaaaaah! (*She's in pain.*) Mustn't get excited.

'As a socialist,' he said. Ha!

Your problem, Betty Lemon, is you never had ambition. Let 'em win, you always used to say. Who can be bothered with all that getting ahead, all that scheming and wheeling and dealing, all that skullduggery and pecking of others out of the way. Let 'em win!

(*Returns to letter.*)

(*Reading*) 'Dress optional . . .'

Options in life are like an inverted pyramid! (*Thinks about it.*) Can't bear people who say things like that.

'As a socialist,' he said. Ha!

Shall I ring my daughter? Tell her the good news? 'Daughter, guess what! Your mother's been honoured. She's been made Handicapped Woman of the Year. I can put HWOY after my name. I'm a Hwoy! Lady Betty Lemon, Hwoy!'

(*Giggles, and drives her chair to lounge where phone sits.*)

Probably just get her answering machine. 'I'm not here.' Only people I ever speak to these days are answering machines. All got their own personalities, though. Some sing, some play music, some make jokes. My daughter's machine is sparse. 'I'm not here.' A machine of few words.

Lady Betty Lemon, Hwoy! (*Giggles.*)

'As a socialist,' he said. Ha!

Coffee-time, I think.

(*She drives to kitchen area. Preparations for making coffee are another of the day's battles, for it is real coffee made from beans which she grinds in a noisy machine, and then filters. It is not possible to carry this out from a sitting position. She has to stand and leave her chair. Her first moves are to see if there is sufficient water in kettle, switch on.*)

'As a socialist,' he said. Ha! He called everybody who disagreed with him a socialist. You only had to complain to my uncle about rent or rates going up and he'd hiss: 'Socialisssst!'

'But, Uncle,' I'd say, because after a while I'd just enjoy winding him up. 'But, Uncle, if cutting profits is a disincentive to industrialists how can cutting wages be an incentive to workers?'

(*Hissing*) 'Socialisssst!'

(*Enjoying herself*) 'Let 'em win!' I'd yell at him.

'Spineless!' he'd yell back, his eyes popping out of his head, the pitch of his voice rising, the words swimming about in his mouth. 'Flabby! Woolly-minded!'

'Let 'em win!'

(*Hissing*) 'Socialisssst!'

(*Crying out to the noose*) And what about those handicapped by ignorant teachers and bigoted parents. What about *them*?

(*Collects packet of coffee beans from fridge.*)

'I'm not here.' Lady Betty Lemon, Hwoy! (*Giggles.*)

(*The chair moves away from her. It is, of course, radio controlled. She watches it with anger.*)

Not you as well?! Come back here! At once! Now!

(*It backs away again. She hobbles towards it. It backs away. She hobbles another step. It backs away. They are developing a relationship.*)

What's the matter, chair? Too heavy for you?

(*Chair moves.*)

Upsetting to have a smelly old woman sitting on you?

(*Chair moves.*)

Well, no one enjoys being sat upon, I can understand that, but we've all been put on this earth to serve a function and you're luckier than most: you know what yours is.

(*It backs away again.*)

Be a good chair, don't give a venerable, crippled old lady a hard time in the evening of her life. I know you were made for better things than wheeling a cantankerous hag around her squalid flat but think of it this way: she's been crowned Handicapped Queen for a night and you're her throne.

(*The chair sidles away.*)

Not convinced?

(*Chair sidles away once more.*)

I'll put my daughter on to you. Woman of few words and much action, my daughter.

(*Chair sidles even further away.*)

You want to get the better of me, don't you? Decrepit, malfunctioning, full of wheezes, but I go on and on and on and on and it makes you mad, eh? She should be dead, you're thinking. Why does she linger? Who's interested in her? Who cares what she does, what she feels, what she thinks'. Get it over and done with! Sing praises! Bury her! Give the barmy old battleaxe a tomb and flowers. Goodbye, Betty Lemon. Farewell, you irritating old fart.

'Rubbish!' he said. 'They all talk rubbish!'

(*An idea occurs to her. Perhaps if she pretends she's not interested in the chair it will stand still. She returns to making coffee.*)

Can't let life's little irritations keep me from my coffee.

(The beans must be poured into grinder. Inevitably they spill into the sink. She meticulously retrieves each bean.)

'As a socialist.' Ha!

Was I ever really a socialist? I *called* myself one in those days because in those days there was no other name for what I believed. But – ssssh! Don't let on. I never joined! Wasn't a joiner. Couldn't accept majority decisions. Never really liked the majority. Not like Sir James. He loved them.

We once went on a goodwill mission to East Germany. Visited a small industrial town. Can't remember the name but I'll never forget the scene. The local councillors gave us a tea. Five of them neatly dressed in suits of lifeless greys and browns and blues on one side of a long table, Sir James and Lady Betty Lemon from Dalston Junction with their interpreter on the other side, and little sandwiches in between all set in a clean, polished, bleak room with photos of grim men on the cream walls. And I remember asking: 'Why are all your left-wing leaders looking to the right?' No one thought that funny. The chief councillor was the first to speak. 'I come from the working class,' he said. 'I love the working class.' It was how he said the word 'love' which fascinated me. Urgently. Anxiously. Protestingly. 'I luuuve the working class, I luuuve them.' Methought he did protest too much, as though warding them. Calming them. He didn't love them. He was terrified of them.

(The beans are in the grinder. Press button. Loud noise. Stop.)

(Crying out to the noose) And what about those handicapped by weak minds? What about *them*?

(She must now pour ground coffee into the small filter pot and pour in hot water.)

They say yesterday's whores are today's nuns. Or is it: Today's nuns were yesterday's whores? Or perhaps it's: Today's whores are tomorrow's nuns? *(Beat.)* Can't bear people who say things like that.

On the other hand, you see those crowds on television and it doesn't matter what country they're in or what they're demonstrating about, their faces all have the same expression – simplistic fervour. Self-intoxicated. No thought. They've persuaded themselves their ends will be achieved now! At this moment! Repeat the screaming, that'll do it. Clench your fist, that'll bring the millennium.

'Rubbish!' he said. 'They all talk rubbish!'

'Ollymollycollywolly OUT OUT OUT! Thingymeejig and wadjama-callim OUT OUT OUT!'

Like a magic incantation. Their eyes ablaze with self-satisfaction. They've made a better world. Today!

'Ollymollycollywolly OUT OUT OUT! Thingymeejig and wadjama-callim OUT OUT OUT!'

While far away alone in a cold land a man lives out his existence frozen for saying, 'No.'

(*Crying out to the noose*) And what about those handicapped by demagogues, charlatans, charismatic politicians? What about them?

(*Pours her coffee. Moves with it towards armchair in study.*)
I fought them, ha! Didn't I fight them? That's why Sir James turned to other women – I saw through him. 'You play to the gallery,' I told him. 'Easy solutions and slick slogans. The politics of comfort! Questions! Questions! You don't teach them to ask questions. You're filled with lies and bullshit,' I told him. 'With rubbish!' (*Beat.*) Not easy to sleep beside a woman who bites the hand that feeds her. (*Puts coffee on desk.*) An anarchist, that's what I really am. Elderly Handicapped Anarchist of the Year, that's me.

'Ollymollycollywolly OUT OUT OUT. Thingymeejig and wadjama-callim OUT OUT OUT!'

(*Lunges with stick at chair which anticipates her and moves away. She falls forward, landing with great pain.*)
You stupid lump of manufacture! Do as you're told! You're not made to have a life of your own, you're made to serve. To serve me! Jesus Christ! Why doesn't anything work as I want it to? Not the chair, not my bowels, not my legs, not memory, not brains! Piss bugger shit fuck, why is nothing easy in this life?!

(*She struggles to lean against desk. Reaches for coffee, drinks.*)
Good coffee. Only the best for the century's cripple.

'My Lords, Ladies and Gentlemen. I wasn't always like this . . .'

Were you not, Betty Lemon? Didn't you always let them win? (*Beat.*) Well, that was the only way to show contempt for the competitors, wasn't it? 'Let 'em win!' I used to drive a car, believe it or believe it not, and there was never a journey without meeting some little smart-arse at the lights who'd grin at me through his window and rev his engine. He wanted to be first off on the yellow, see! What did you do, Lady Lemon? You revved to make him *think* you were competing and then when the lights changed you stayed stock still. Made the little smart-arse really smart.

(*Crying out to the noose*) Let 'em win! Let the relentless silly buggers win!

'I'm not here.' Lady Betty Lemon, Hwoy!

(*A memory strikes her.*)

Thirteen-year-olds! They were only pathetic little thirteen-year-olds. Life still bewildered them. I can see them. They keep looking to the side, checking they're doing it right. And what are they doing? Training to die! Thirteen-year-olds. Their noses are running, their eyes bulge. I can see them. On the TV screen. Some fanatical religious war in the Middle East. Listen to their officers. 'They're not afraid to die because when they die it'll only be for a short time.' Don't believe me? Listen. 'This life is only a preparation. The real one is to follow. They will be instant martyrs in heaven.' Fucking hallelujah! Thank Christ the grave is silent. You can invent what you like – heaven, hell, new lives, new beginnings. And there they stand. Thirteen-year-olds! In rows of three. Blazing eyes. Clenched fists. Fervour. (*Peering*) Except . . . except (*points*) him! That little one there. Look at him. (*Becomes excited as though at a race track.*) He doesn't believe them. He's pulled away. Backed up against a wall. He's crying. 'No! No! Not me! Not me!' Go on, little one. Cry! Cry for your life! Tell them! 'Not me! Not me! Rubbish! You all talk rubbish!'

I shall never forget that picture. *He* wasn't a joiner. Little mite. They should have a dinner for him.

Wonder what his name was? Wonder if they made him go? Wonder if he died, went to heaven?

(*Clock strikes the half.*)

(*She utters, gently, like a lamentation for the dead*) Ollymollycollywolly out out out. Thingymeejig and wadjamacallim out out out.

(*Angrily crying at the noose*) And what about those handicapped by fear of their priests? What about *them*?

You won't go to heaven, Lady Betty Lemon. Too much bile and blasphemy burning you up. No reverence for anything.

(*She rouses herself. The chair moves towards her as though in*

*sympathy. She stretches her arm to greet it. Grateful. It backs away
again. She ignores it with dignity and sits in armchair.)*

Well, there goes another half-hour I won't ever be able to live again.
(*Beat.*) Can't bear people who say things like that.

'My Lords, Ladies and Gentlemen, my life was spent on many
battle fronts . . .'

(*To noose*) If only they'd known my father. He wasn't one of the
world's joiners, either. 'Ach!' he'd say. 'They all talk rubbish and
make me sick.' Dalston Junction was full of people who talked rubbish
and made him sick. 'Separate them into individuals,' he said. 'They're
nicer. Collect them together and you have collective madness.'
Probably inherited my dislike of the majority from him. Lovely man.
Everything hurt him.

(*Shakes herself from reverie . . .*)

'My Lords, Ladies and Gentlemen. I had a father – yes, even old
women may once have had fathers – I had a father who advised me to
be a writer and write rubbish. "Write rubbish," he advised. "Write
rubbish, make a fortune and keep us in our old age." But I didn't want
to be a writer, not even one who made a fortune writing rubbish. I
wanted to be, believe me or believe me not, a runner. Yes! Once I
could run. Once I could swim, dive, the high jump, the long jump,
leap over hurdles – an athlete! That's what I wanted to be, my Lords,
Ladies and Gentlemen, not a writer but a runner who won races. I was
neither. I became a wife. To Sir James.'

(*Crying out to the noose*) What about those handicapped by the
wrong relationship until death do them part. What about *them*?

(*She thinks she hears something.*)

What was that? I heard a voice. There was movement. Who's there?
Is that you, Mother? She always said she'd come back.

'And when I do, don't be frightened.' Why not? Why shouldn't I be
frightened? Give me one good reason why I shouldn't be frightened?

(*Long pause.*)

She once threw a pile of spoons at me. She did! We're sitting down to
a meal and she asks me to go upstairs and bring down two chairs to the
table. My brothers are there and I ask her, 'Why don't they bring them
down?' 'Because I asked *you*,' she replies. 'Well, I won't,' I say. 'Not
while there are two big hefty boys standing idle either side of me.' So
she throws the spoons.

(*She looks around, listens.*)

Mother, are you carrying spoons? I don't really believe she's out there. Or that anyone is out there. That's another of your problems, Betty Lemon, you're not a believer.

(*Phone rings. She struggles to her feet knowing she won't make it in time, cursing like a child.*)

Piss bugger shit fuck! Piss bugger shit fuck! Piss bugger shit fuck!

(*She makes it to the phone just as it stops ringing.*)

Probably my daughter. She always rings when I'm otherwise engaged. Does it deliberately. 'Mother's moving her bowels, let's ring her.'

(*She dials. Waits. We hear the phone ring followed by the whirr of a machine going into action. Her daughter's recorded voice over.*)

DAUGHTER'S VOICE

I'm not here. If –

(BETTY *slams down phone angrily.*)

BETTY

Of course you're not there! Can't I hear you're not fucking there! She's worked out this message specially to annoy me. No: 'This is 262 2134' so's you know you've got the right number. No: 'I'm sorry we're not here' or 'I'm sorry we're working' or 'I'm sorry we're not in the mood for speaking to people.' Nothing!

'They know my voice,' she says.

'But what if someone needs you urgently who doesn't know your voice?'

(*She dials again.*)

DAUGHTER'S VOICE

I'm not here. If you want to leave a message speak after the tone.

(*Tone.* BETTY *replaces receiver.*)

BETTY

Not even: '*Please* speak after the tone and I'll ring you back.' Sparse. She's very sparse, my daughter. Now *she* wants to be a writer. A sparse writer.

(*Crying out to the noose*) What about those handicapped by talent, taste, a touch of colour, style? What about *them*?

(*Imitating the diminishers*) 'Who does she think she is? Takes herself too seriously, that's her trouble.'

'Write rubbish,' I yell at her. 'Write rubbish and make a fortune and keep me in my old age.' Not her.

'I'm not here.' Uncompromising. 'I'm not here.' A sparse writer. 'I'm not here.' You can't be more sparse than that.

(*Dials again.*)

DAUGHTER'S VOICE

I'm not here. If you want to leave a message speak after the tone.

BETTY

Hello, machine. And how are *you* today? (*Beat.*) Can't talk? Not feeling well? Feeling depressed? Well, one thing you'll never have to endure: speaking into the fucking void.

Hello, daughter. This is your handicapped mother of the year calling you from heaven. I passed away two months ago. You can reach me on cloud nine extension 010101010101 . . . Oh! Oh! Oh?

(*She is in tears. Controls herself.*)

Goodbye, machine.

(*Receiver down.*)

(*Calling out to the noose*) And what about those handicapped by despair? What about *them*?

(*She wanders around her flat. Lost. Lonely. Uncertain what to do, where to settle. Finds herself beneath the noose. Utterly depressed.*)

One thing I never was – sparse. There was something mean about being sparse – a tight-lipped malice, a thin envy, a grudging rebuke. I was never grudging, envious, mean. Touch of malice now and then, can't help that in this life, but – careful? Never. Sir James was. Trod carefully. Loved carefully. Carefully approved of and hated the right people, the charmed groups, the beloved causes. Not a hair or a word out of place, not a decibel above par. Me – I chased and screamed him around the globe, took emotional risks, asked unfashionable questions. Fatal! Loud and lavish in a steely, sparse land. Fatal! But to him they gave a knighthood. (*Beat.*) And kept him out of the Cabinet. My fault. All my fault. Everything my fault. I let 'em win.

'My Lords, Ladies and Gentlemen. I had a mother – yes, even old women may once have had mothers – I had a mother, a strong and tiny thing she was who gave me two pieces of advice. "Talk," she said. "Always say it. Something is remembered." And once, when I was rude and she was upset, I told her, "But I was only joking."

'"There are no jokes. Nobody", she said, "makes jokes."'

(*Slowly an idea comes to her. She raises her stick to pull down noose. She is going to use it to lasso her wheelchair! What follows depends*

upon the power for comic invention of the actress and director.
Whatever that is, she finally succeeds. The chair is hers again. She
circles the space in a kind of triumphant lap of honour. The feeling of
triumph is brief.)

'My Lords, Ladies and Gentlemen. I wasn't always like this. I . . .'

'My Lords, Ladies and Gentlemen. My life was spent on many battle fronts which . . .'

'My Lords, Ladies and Gentlemen. We are given but one life, and . . .'

'My Lords, Ladies and Gentlemen . . . I didn't fucking plan it this way.'

(*Whirring clock strikes eight. Slow fade of lights.*)

FOUR PORTRAITS – OF MOTHERS

Four Portraits – Of Mothers was written for the Tokyo Festival of One-act Plays. It was first performed on 2 July 1982 at the Mitzukoshi Royal Theatre, Tokyo, by Michiko Otsuka, directed by Tsunetoshi Hirowatari. Its United Kingdom premiere took place during the Edinburgh Festival on 20 August 1984 at the Netherbow Theatre, Edinburgh, when it was performed by Anne Lacey, directed by Donald Smith. The first London performance was on 20 October 1987 at the Half Moon Theatre, given by Anne Chauveau, directed by Valerie Cogan, designed by Paul Minter.

WOMAN AS UNMARRIED MOTHER
RUTH, aged thirty-nine

WOMAN AS MOTHER WHO NEVER WAS
NAOMI, aged seventy, Jewish

WOMAN AS FAILED MOTHER
MIRIAM, aged forty-five

WOMAN AS MOTHER EARTH
DEBORAH, aged thirty-five

I imagine that for each character the actress will add or discard one or two garments, perhaps a wig, perhaps a small prop, to help. But the portrayals will depend mainly upon acting. It should not matter if the actress is and looks thirty-five when she is portraying a much older woman. The challenge in these vignettes is to convey an *impression* of the personalities, through timbre and pace of voice, and through physical gestures, especially such as the folding of clothes by Ruth.

Each setting is indicated by one or two pieces of furniture. All are visible on the stage. The actress moves into each one for her different portrayal. Except for the supermarket – in this scene she can push her trolley all around the stage in a circular movement, reaching up and down into space for her shopping.

A.W.

RUTH

A bed, two suitcases on it, a pile of clothes beside each, and a huge stuffed monkey.

RUTH *is packing for a holiday, and talking, in mock anger, to her child, unseen in another room.*

RUTH

(*Calling*) And I'll tell you something else, Divine Brat, I may love and adore you but I'm not packing your case. I'm packing my own case but yourn will remain unpacked by anyone but *you*!

(*To herself*) Does she imagine I've built up this business so's she can sit on her pretty little bum and complain of the world's cruelty? Well, I haven't!

(*Calling*) Do you imagine I've built up this business so's you can sit on your pretty little bum and complain of the world's cruelty? Well, I haven't!

(*To herself*) It's a hard world run by men who are frightened of women, and I'm going to make certain she's independent of them.

(*Calling*) I want you to learn everything – from threading a needle to cooking a dinner, from running a career to packing a case! It's a hard world run by men who are frightened of women, and I'm going to make certain you're independent of them.

(*To herself*) She's got me repeating myself. I'm going mad. She'll lose me to the asylum!

(*Calling*) So you don't have a father! I'm a criminal! You've told me a thousand times. *I'm* tired of hearing it and *you* should be tired of telling it, now come and help me pack. It's our first skiing holiday and we have to think carefully about what we take or we'll freeze.

(*To herself*) I'm tolerating no nonsense from her. Children! You never win! If I'd have married he'd've been the wrong father; if he'd been the right father I'd've been the wrong mother; if we'd both been right she'd've said our happiness was excluding her! Well, if she thinks I'm going to encourage self-pity she's got another think coming!

Two sweaters, or four? For a change? Four! And you can be certain I'll leave behind the only one I care about.

(*Pause. Listening*) Yes, I know, fathers are important. But lesson number one: no one is indispensable. Lesson number two: face reality, don't succumb to it. And lesson number three: girls who cry miss planes. (*Pause.*) What do you mean, the last one's a proverb? Are you trying to teach me the difference between a lesson and a proverb?

(*To herself*) Bloody kids! They'll even stop crying to point out your mistakes. And I've got plenty and doesn't she know them and doesn't she tell me them?

(*Calling*) And what's so special about men anyway? You think *I* can't teach you to ski? You think *I* can't make campfires? You think *I* can't giggle and horseplay in the snow?

(*To herself*) She's right! I can't! I hate skiing, and I hate snow, and I hate all that cold and those hearty, healthy, rosy-cheeked people. Especially healthy rose-cheeked women. And what's more I hate being *alone* on holiday with her. But what can I do, for God's sake! *I* didn't purchase a husband, *she* hasn't inherited a father, and that's that.

And there's the question of what books to take, and games. Or do they have games there? I don't know. What do I know? What do I know about skiing resorts, except they're places where you break legs?

(*Calling*) A father's expensive, anyway. He *spends* his money on possessions, he *takes* up most of the space, *you* end up revolving around *his* needs, and before you know it *you're* made to feel guilty for imprisoning *him*! Trust me, Divine Brat, we'll find a temporary father on the slopes. You'll fall, I'll weep, they'll come running!

(*To herself*) Full of consolation, masculine protectiveness, and suppressed fantasies. God! I hate them! (*Pause.*) God! I need them. (*Pause.*) God! I hate myself for needing them! (*Pause.*) I must be crazy. A skiing holiday! The world slips under my feet every day, why should I wear skis to help it!

Foolish girl! Does she imagine I don't need a partner for myself as much as she needs a dad? (*Pause.*) Well, not *all* the time, but just now and then, when I'm on heat, or when she's hating me. Hired! Like cars by the hour! For a day or a week! I mean, it wouldn't be so bad if we could hire them for just a year, and then take them back, like a

40

library book you've finished reading. After all, no man is an *endless* book!

(*Calling*) That's a proverb for you: no man is an endless book!

(*To herself*) And I knew *that* from the start, as though God had singled me out for protection! Ruth, he warned me, no man is an endless book. (*Pause.*) Besides, I wanted to be dependent on *no* one. No one! (*Pause.*) That's an absurd thing to say. Live alone and you talk nonsense to yourself – no one to contradict you! No one is ever independent. If I needed no one else I'd need *her*. The Divine Brat!

(*Calling*) Hey, Divine Brat! You made a list, there's an empty case waiting to be filled up, now come and do it. Please! If you don't pull yourself together you'll have to ski naked, and frozen pubic hairs are rough on the skin.

(*To herself*) She didn't find it funny. Well, it wasn't very funny but that's no reason not to laugh. I'm her mother. She's supposed to humour me. No sense of humour! My daughter has no sense of humour! Children are by nature morbid, give them something to be sad about and at once they're happy.

(*Calling*) Hey! Did I ever tell you how the world knows Jesus was Jewish? One: He didn't leave home till he was thirty-five. Two: *He* thought *she* was a virgin. Three: *She* thought *he* was God! (*Pause.*) I made a joke! Your terrible mother made a joke! Laugh, for God's sake. It may not happen again.

(*Waits. No response.*)

What more can I do for you? I work for you, shop for you, plot for you, cook for you, I bleed for you, wash for you, long for you, weep for you, ache for you . . . (*picks up stuffed monkey and dances with it*) . . . and I dance, dance, dance, dance, daaaaaaaance for you!

(*Flops on bed.*)

(*To herself*) I'm a performing idiot! That's what mothers are, performing idiots!

(*Calling*) Mothers are performing idiots!

(*To herself*) What kind of respect can I expect? Wallop her, that's what I should do. That's what a good father would do. She wants a father? Right! I'll show her what a father is. (*Wailing like a child*) 'I want a daddy.' Wallop! 'I won't go to school.' Wallop! 'I don't want to go skiing.' Wallop! She doesn't want to be happy? Intelligent?

Independent? Self-sufficient? Strong? Wallop! Wallop! Wallop wallop wallop!

(*Calling*) Divine Brat! Come here and be walloped.

(*To herself*) Wouldn't do any good. Last time I walloped her it was me who cried. (*Pause.*) But she's right. Times like these you need a man. Damn them! Damn them, damn them, damn them! (*Pause.*) Ignore her, that's what I'll do.

(*Calling*) I'm ignoring you! I'm packing my cases and if you don't pack yours then there'll be the usual last-minute rush and you'll have to leave half of what you need behind because there won't be time to look for it because it'll all be buried in those corners of the flat you manage to find and I never knew existed and I'll get the blame because when it suits you I'm the older more responsible member of this family SO COME THIS INSTANT WHEN I CALL YOU!

(*To herself, complete change of mood*) Besides, I grabbed my chance. Who would've wanted to marry me? Plain, graceless, difficult, clever. Impossible combination for a man to accept. Could hardly get one to talk to me let alone sleep with me! And to marry me? Never! So I saw this man and I said to myself – 'him!' Paid a fortune to be made up, used all my will-power to be gracious and tried hard not to be clever. Result? The Divine Brat!

(*Calling*) You, Divine Brat!

(*To herself*) She'll think I've gone mad.

(*Begins to pack daughter's case.*)

And it was worth every tear of it. Every humiliation, every lie, every struggle. *She* was what I wanted. Exactly. The way she looks, the way she thinks, the way she feels, the way she loves, quarrels, smiles, blackmails, teases, sings, dances, questions, observes, screams, cries, perseveres. Perseveres? Stubborn, more like. What am I doing? I'm packing her case. Look at me! I'm giving in to her again.

(*Calling*) Divine Stubborn Brat! Come here! *You* may need your daddy but your mother needs *you*.

(*She opens her arms. Waits.*)

(*To herself*) But don't you ever take advantage of that, Divine Brat, not ever.

(*Smiles. The child is coming. Slow fade.*)

NAOMI

Four features distinguish NAOMI'*s personality: a paperback book, which she has read so many times that all its pages are loose, but she continually reaches for it to read a sentence or two, as though needing to stay in touch with something familiar and loved; the song she hums every so often, a Negro lullaby 'O ma babby, ma curly-headed babby'. It's an unconscious humming. Third, a constant need for 'news', about anything! Finally, her habit of sitting in her armchair with one leg cocked over an arm.*

She sits in a faded leather armchair leaning against a tatty, crocheted cover, made long ago by herself. She will sit in this armchair throughout.

A small, round table covered by a faded cloth is at her side. On it is the paperback book, a dusty telephone, an opened egg in its cup, some fingers of toast, a cup of tea, jug of milk, sugar bowl. At her side, on the floor, is a pot of tea and a tin of biscuits. On the television is a dead pot plant. The atmosphere is one of resignation and neglect.

As lights go up the television is on but sound is down. NAOMI *is fumbling with her broken paperback book; she has to turn a page and as all the leaves are loose she's having difficulty. It is our first image of her.*

She reads, eyes close to the page. Sighs. Replaces book. Sips from her cup of tea. Pauses to look at outside of the cup, something stuck to it. She scratches it away. Yesterday's crumbs! Shrugs. Drinks again.

Now she faces television set. Hums and gazes. Then, realizing there's no sound, she leans forward to turn it up louder. Sits.

And sits.

Phone rings. Seems not to hear it. Then does.

NAOMI

Hello?

Oh hello, Danny.

All right, thank you. Any news?

What?

I can't hear you, this is a terrible line. What did you say?

Wait a minute.

(*She leans forward to turn down television.*)

Hello?

That's better.

(*She pours herself out another cup of tea, reaches for biscuit tin at*

*her side which she places between her knees in order to pull off the lid,
takes out biscuits, replaces lid and box, dips biscuit into tea. It has all
been done with one hand, the other holds the phone; she's talking
meanwhile.)*

I'm watching television.

No, there's never anything worthwhile. I just switch it on and
think of other things. Any news?

What was that?

I can't hear you.

Yes, I've had my supper, thank you.

A boiled egg and toasted fingers with butter.

Because I can't be bothered to make anything more. Besides I have
a good lunch.

Some meat and cheese and a banana.

It's enough. What more do I need!

What?

I can't hear you.

Yes, the flat's clean.

Yes, I've dusted.

No, I'll Hoover tomorrow.

Tomorrow, tomorrow, I'll Hoover tomorrow. Stop nagging. Any
news?

I'm not shouting. Any news?

David is what?

No, my ears don't need syringing. I keep telling you, it's a bad line.
David is what?

Leaving his job? What's he going to do?

What?

Travel? Where's he going to travel?

'Everywhere' is a big place. What's he going to use for money?

Well, he won't get far on that, will he?

You 'what' for him?

I can't hear, say it again.

Oh, this is a shocking line, shocking. You 'what' for him?

A.

B.

What?

E?

44

Oh, C. Yes, A – C –
H.
D?
What?
B.

Oh, E. A – C – H – E. You 'ache' for him. Well aching won't do much good, he's got to go through it himself, learn the hard way like we all did, only some of us didn't learn, and some of us who did learned too late.

You want me to do what?

To speak to who?

You want me to speak to Abe Border? Who's Abe Border?

Oh, you want me to speak into a tape recorder. What for?

Don't be a silly boy, Danny. I can't remember all those years back. And anyway, who wants to? I miss nothing. It was all terrible. My childhood was terrible, my youth was terrible, I missed a married life, which I knew some people would say was not so terrible but I'd like to have decided for myself, and here I am. No one in the middle of nowhere with no more chances. Nothing good to remember, nothing good to miss.

All right, you'll come when you'll come. I'm not going anywhere.

Yes, you too. Thank you for calling.

I promise, I promise, I'll Hoover tomorrow.

> (*Replaces phone. Looks sadly around. Runs her finger over top of television and wipes dust on her apron. The exchange has made her sad. She reaches out for the book. Fumbles and reads. Sighs. Replaces book. Returns to watching television without turning up the sound. Hums to herself. Then –*)

'Tell me what you miss from those years, tell me what you remember from those years.' Silly boy! What can I remember? My memory's gone to sleep. I looked after an invalid mother, then I looked after a sick sister and now there's no one to look after me – *that's* what I remember. A life gone! No sodding justice in this world.

> (*Hums. Then –*)

I suppose it could wake up, my memory, if Prince Charming came along.

> (*The thought amuses her and she giggles. It is a special, innocent moment, full of old-age charm.*)

Prince Charming!
    (*Hums. Then –*)
I remember once, a Christmas time, it was when we were living in the East End, still young girls, and all the other children were talking about their Christmas stocking, and how it was going to be filled. Of course it was really pillow cases they hung up cos you couldn't get much into a stocking, could you? So I thought, well, I'll also try it, see what happens. Jewish people don't celebrate Christmas but maybe Father Christmas couldn't tell the difference between Jews and Christians. I'd take a chance! So I hung up a huge pillow case and when I woke on Christmas morning I rushed to look and found – it was empty!

    It's been like that ever since.
    (*Phone rings. She leans to pick it up.*)
Hello, Danny? Twice in one day? You've got a little news for me?
    What?
    You feel low? What are *you* low about?
    About me? Don't worry about me, worry about yourself and your family, I'm all right. I just had a good laugh.
    About Prince Charming. (*Giggles.*)
    Explain! Explain! How can I explain? Tell me some news instead.
    Well, what can you do! I'm an old woman who had no children, and that's what happens to old women who have no children: they grow old with no children. Now think of some news to tell me.
    I'm watching a comedy show.
    I know it's a terrible show but I put it on to hear a human voice.
    Well, it's true, isn't it? You ring me and that's good of you but yours is the only voice I hear.
    I'm not sad.
    I'm *not* sad.
    I'm not *sad*! I've just had the stuffing knocked out of me and that's that. Stop worrying, and think of some news to tell me. It'll soon be over, besides.
    No, I'm not trying to depress you. I'm facing reality. How much longer do you think I've got?
    What?
    What?
    Ten or fifteen years? Oh, Danny! Don't be wicked. You wish me ten

or fifteen more years of *this*? Don't be wicked! I'm not wicked to you.

No, I've already told you. I've dusted today and I'll Hoover tomorrow.

I promise.

Yes, tomorrow. I'll Hoover tomorrow.

You're a good nephew.

I promise.

Tomorrow.

Bye.

(*Phone down. She reaches for her book. Fumbles. Reads. Replaces it. Watches silent screen.*)

'Dust,' he tells me, 'and Hoover! A little bit each day!' If I had someone to Hoover for, I'd Hoover! 'Do it yourself,' he says. 'It'll raise your spirits!' Spirits! It's enough I get up in the mornings. 'Remember, you're a senior citizen,' he says. Humbug! I'm not a senior citizen, I'm a very dried-up tired old woman. 'Are you a middle-aged citizen?' I ask him. 'Do you call your children junior citizens? Young is young, and old is old,' I tell him. 'Don't insult me!'

(*She leans forward to the flickering screen, runs a finger over a part of it. Then she rubs the same spot. And again, more vigorously. Finally, she takes her handkerchief, spits on it, and cleans the entire screen. When she's finished she looks at it in amazement; it shines brightly back at her.*)

Now that really *was* dirt.

(*She looks slowly around the room as though realizing for the first time how she's allowed it all to go to pieces. She reaches for the dead pot plant, gazes at it sadly, a symbol of her self-neglect. Replaces it. Settles back in the armchair, one leg cocked over the arm. Hums. Stops. Shivers, a sudden chill runs through her. She hugs herself. Hums. Stops.*)

What I really miss is to be held. No one's held me for years. Not for years and years. Imagine!

(*Hums. Stops.*)

Wish he'd've been *my* son.

(*Pause. Hums. Lights slow fade.*)

MIRIAM

MIRIAM *is smartly dressed. She's talking to a psychiatrist.*

MIRIAM

It begins with a scream. But it's not mine. I was just born with it. Like a pea in an empty tin can, it rattles when I try to move. No! The wrong image. Like a tumour, growing as I grow. No! Not that, either. It doesn't grow, it diminishes. And it's not *in* me. I am it, someone else's scream, but diminished, like an echo. (*Pause.*) Who knows?

My mother was unworldly.

Do you know what it's costing me to sit before you and say all this? Do you know with what confidence and happiness and expectation I entered marriage and motherhood? The plans I had, the theories I'd read, the careful thought that went into those girls? I couldn't wait to have children. Do you know that?

Some women want happy husbands as their monument, some fight for careers, or plan wealth, or scheme for status. But not me. My monument was to be my children. (*Pause.*) Who knows?

My mother was unworldly.

You think that was the cause for the mess, don't you? I wanted it for *my* sake and not theirs. It looks like that, doesn't it? But it's not true. Not if you look at what actually happened: I didn't have special ambitions for them. It wasn't that I wanted one to be a doctor, another to be a film star, another to run a business. Of course that would have been lovely – security, glory, a sense of achievement. And why not? But no. Instead I said, 'I don't care what you do as long as you're happy'!

'Happy'! 'I don't care what you do'! Sentimental nonsense! I cared all right, but I pretended I didn't. What I should have done is pushed them, urged, nagged, scolded. But no, I thought, if I show too much concern they'll react against my nagging.

And who knows, perhaps they would have done. Some children have natures so perverse they'll only act by opposites. (*Pause.*) Who knows?

My mother was unworldly.

On the other hand some mothers can never do right. No matter what they do they strike the wrong note. Perhaps *that's* what was wrong. My style. All people have style, don't they? When you say about somebody, 'Oh, *they* can get away with murder', you mean they can do the wrong thing and it works, while some of us, even when we do the right thing, do it badly. Perhaps that was me: the wrong person to be right. Some of us are like that. We're just the wrong people to be right. God knows!

My style? (*Pause.*) Style, style, style! (*Pause.*) Echoes. Diminished echoes.

My mother was unworldly.

Do you realize how humiliating I find it to talk to a psychoanalyst? The ultimate defeat! Well, how else can it be interpreted? Your friends have no resources, your family have no resources, and you have no resources. All known human sympathy and comprehension sucked dry. So – the shrink! The last resort before whom you must confess, wail, weep, reveal, betray.

No, I'm not going to betray my husband. It's tempting to blame him but I won't. We were together in all this. I don't mean we agreed, I mean we shared the responsibility. In fact we *didn't* agree. He wanted to shout and slap them when they misbehaved. I wouldn't let him. Can't bear coarseness, violence, shouting. Talk! Reason! Explain!

I was wrong, wasn't I? Not all misbehaviour is explicable.

Yes, it is! Pleasure! Misbehaviour provides pleasure. (*Thinks about this.*) Can such pleasures be talked, reasoned, explained away? Thwart it and you have violence, don't you? (*Pause.*) Who knows?

My mother was unworldly.

But it was unacceptable pleasure and I failed to let them know it was unacceptable. Sometimes you should shout. Show your anger, your outrage. Outrage is important. I lost my capacity for outrage, *that* was the problem. I confused outrage for moral righteousness. (*Pause.*) Though I never did know what was wrong with a little moral righteousness. I was made to feel ashamed to express it, but I could have afforded an occasional slap. But there! It was not in me. I couldn't. Could I help my nature? My nature? (*Pause.*) My nature, nature, nature! (*Pause.*) Echoes. Diminished echoes. (*Pause, angrily*) Unworldly! That's what I was, unworldly! I didn't understand the world, couldn't piece it together. And I still don't, and I still can't!

Why? Why? Why? Damn it, why? Others could. Others made perfect sense of it, but not me. Not *me*!

(*Pause.*)

My mother was unworldly.

(*Pause.*)

But I prevented my husband from showing *his* anger, and that was wrong, wasn't it? It's good to be different, providing you give people space for it.

Space! The secret to all relationships, isn't it? Husband and wife, friend and friend, state and individual, parent and child – space! Each must be allowed their proper space.

So they were badly brought up, my poor daughters. Yanked up through life by one arm instead of two, because I didn't allow their father to be what he is. I didn't give him his space.

Not true! He didn't allow their mother to be what *she* is! He didn't give me *my* space.

Why didn't he? Why didn't I?

Why? Why? (*Pause.*) Who knows?

My mother was unworldly.

I'm not even the original scream. My whole life is just an echo of someone else's echo whose life was an echo of someone else's echo, whose life was an echo of an echo of an echo of an echo of an echo of an echo . . .

But *who* was the scream?

My poor girls. Echoes! Thin echoes! And each echo becomes thinner.

(*Pause. She utters a loud scream. It seems not to come from her. Blackout.*)

DEBORAH

DEBORAH *wheels a supermarket trolley around, reaching up for this, down for that, and talking to another housewife at her side.*

She's energetic, defiant, full of delight in her life.

Electronic sound of cash register constantly in background.

DEBORAH

Me a prisoner? Never! Those poor men, tied to their jobs, tied to their hours, caught in a rush to a top they'll never reach in a thousand years – they're the prisoners, they're the slaves! But not me! I enjoy the freedom of my home too much.

Look out for the date on that yoghurt. (*Calls to assistant*) Young man! Take this batch away. They're past the sell-by date. (*To neighbour*) Mustn't let them get away with anything.

Yes, I have three of them, and if it wasn't so tiring and costly and boring to be married to a woman who was always fat and pregnant I'd have a dozen of them! Love them! Everything about them. I loved carrying them, giving birth to them, suckling them. I loved changing their smelly nappies, washing their smelly bums with smelly soap, oiling their chapped skin with smelly oils, powdering their fat bodies with smelly powders – all of it! Every smelly second of it! It's what I always wanted to do, what I still want to do, and what I'm supremely equipped to do. So just let anyone dare bully me into thinking it's me who's the prisoner.

Don't buy that! Frozen pastry! Doesn't work. Makes your pies taste like leather. I made a meat pie from it last week and it felt as though we were eating *viande à la* old boot! Make your own. Better! Get the feel of that flour and butter in your hands. Lovely! Like kneading a man's bum. Lovely!

I mean I'd *always* wanted to marry, always wanted to have children, always wanted two boys and one girl and that's what I got! Born lucky! Everything fell into place. Just as I'd dreamed.

Oh, look! This week's special offer. Candles! I'm mad about candles. I burn them all the time. From the moment I get up I light a candle so's to have a moving flame in front of me. Some people hate them. Reminds them of death. Not me! 'Someone's at home!' it says. 'A person's around, waiting, preparing, looking out for you!' If I had my way I'd live by candlelight, and heat by firelight.

Now *that's* a good buy. Three packets of meat for the price of two. You can stock up for a couple of weeks with that. Why don't you take some pork, beef, and lamb – one of them's free!

No escaping the fact – I'm a shopper! I love shopping. I don't mean I'm the sort to go a mile to save a penny, but I love abundance. And don't get me wrong when I say that. My children are not spoilt or overfed. They know about poverty, they know about hard work, and they know everything has to be earned. *And* all the dictionaries and encyclopaedias are there on the shelves to help them: science and music, rivers and religions, phrases and fables, etymology, mythology, anthropology – everything! Everything's on offer in our house. They can reach to any shelf and learn about where they came from. There's even a dictionary of chivalry, because I want them polite, grateful and conscious of the difficult world they live in – but! Oh! The pleasure I get seeing them eat a good meal, the reward to see them feel confident. I don't want them smug but I do want them courageous. And generous. I can't bear meanness of any sort. Abundance! Spiritually, intellectually, emotionally. I love abundance.

Now *there's* something you ought to try. It's not cheap but it's a real delicacy. Something to surprise them with. Made in Denmark. An absolutely scrumptious biscuit. Melts in your mouth.

Sorry! But what can I do? I enjoy feeding people. In fact I've often thought that I'd hire myself out for a fee as a shopper. There are some people, you know, who hate shopping. Simply hate it. Not me. I bet I could earn quite a living doing other people's shopping. Fancy! Being paid to do something you like. How I'd love to spend other people's money stocking up all the things I couldn't afford myself. That would really be exciting, like living other people's lives. Paid to be everybody's mother. Ha!

Now if you'll listen to me you'll take those soaps on offer. I saw them fifty pence more in the chemist yesterday. French soaps. Lovely!

I get very angry when people ask what I do and I tell them and they say, 'Oh, you don't have a profession, then?' I *do* have a profession. A very skilful profession. A profession full of different skills. Not only cooking, washing, ironing, but organizing. People don't realize the organization that goes into running a household. Budgeting, stocking up, planning ahead. And the imagination that's required! All those details that make my home a haven, a womb, an anchor, a magnet! I don't want them to take me for granted but I do want them to be certain of me. That gives me a great satisfaction that does, to be relied upon. I'm there! I'm willing! I begrudge no effort! And the result is I've made a place no one ever wants to leave. A treasure house full of little goodies in cupboards, snacks in the fridge, crisp sheets on the bed once a week, different soaps, copper shining on the walls, shelves and leather dusted and smelling of pine, always a clean shirt, a fresh hot towel, a home-cooked meal. And to remind them of nature the house is covered with pot plants creeping and crawling all over the place which I water and prune and talk to.

And if my husband wasn't allergic to animal smells I'd have lots of animals roaming around like lion cubs and koala bears. I'm needed, wanted, depended upon. I glory in it, bathe in it, thrive on it!

Me the prisoner? Never!

(*Blackout.*)

THE MISTRESS

This is a pre-production version of *The Mistress*, the last of the cycle, written between 15 and 27 June 1988.

On Passover night the youngest child asks, 'Wherefore is this night different from all other nights? . . .' And the father replies, 'Once were we slaves in Egypt, and the Lord our God brought us forth from thence with a mighty hand and an outstretched arm . . .'

A dress designer's atelier.

Although there is an office area – desk, chair, phone – the main atmosphere is created by the paraphernalia of the workshop: four sewing machines; an overlock machine fed by coons of coloured nylon thread which stretch across space like a Hepworth sculpture; ironing board; cutting table; racks upon which hang finished clothes; garments in various stages of completion outlined against a wall; rolls of cloth and lining on shelves; a battery of pegs on which are 'plugged' cotton reels of every possible hue; drawings, sketches, cuttings from fashion magazines pinned on boards; and two tailor's dummies draped in startling but unfinished dresses.

The atmosphere of this workshop is flushed by shape, texture and a mosaic blaze of colour.

Two mottoes printed boldly on separate boards give us the first hint of the woman we are about to see:

KNOCK HARD. LIFE IS DEAF

NO GOOD DEED GOES UNPUNISHED.

SAMANTHA MILNER *enters with a pile of magazines in her arms, dressed in what could be described as the 'Russian' look: voluminous skirt, embroidered blouse, peasant waistcoat, boots. Obviously her own creation. On the end of her nose – thick, black-rimmed glasses.*

She is thirty-nine years old, voluptuous, energetic, efficient, talented and famous. Her parents were Eastern European emigrés but she has no accent. Just a rhythm of speech.

SAMANTHA

(*To the dummies*) Good evening, girls!

> (*Where to put the magazines in all this clutter? For the moment – the cutting table.*)

My, but you look beautiful this evening. Where *did* you get those stunning dresses?

> (*Approaches one to make an alteration.*)

Are we going to have a nice quiet evening together? Catch up on work? Answer the appeal letters? No insolence, no back-chat, no blinding questions?

You're talking to the dummies, Sam. You promised yourself you'd *stop* talking to the dummies, Sam.

She promised herself many things didn't she, Jessica? To stop drinking, to cut out chocolates, to say 'no' more often to clients, to give him up.

(*All innocent*) To give who up?

Him, Samantha, him! 'Who'! God, you're so full of shit.

(*Steps back to view her work.*)

There! Better! Better, Jessica? Better!

(*Turns to second dummy.*)

You, Ninotchka, I'm *not* so sure about. You looked good on the drawing board but on your feet? No, don't cry. It's probably something very simple. (*Beat.*) Like starting from scratch.

(*Moves to a drawing pad. Flicks through pages. A drawing catches her eye. She raises pad away from her. Considers it. Something wrong. She takes a pencil to it. Makes changes. Worse! Puts a huge X across the page.*)

Cursi!* Cursi, cursi, cursi!

(*The phone rings. She stiffens but doesn't move. Looks at her watch.*)

That's not you. It can't be you. You're too early.

(*It rings on.*)

You're a client. A rich, impatient, thoughtlessly demanding client who forgot she has a wedding in two days' time and needs an outfit.

(*It rings on.*)

It *can't* be you. (*Pause.*) You're a client inviting me to one of your hen parties. I don't like hen parties. You'll talk about your diets, your husbands, your children, your homes in that order and I'm not interested. I am *not*!

(*Phone stops.*)

Thank you. (*Pause.*) Or *was* it you? Christ! We make plans, maps, sign codes, language codes, time schedules, and invent one-act plays with imaginary dialogue and still nothing is predictable!

(*Phone rings again.*)

It *can't* be you!

(*It rings on.*)

You're a client on my blacklist ringing to apologize for passing me a dud cheque. (*Beat.*) Or the one who tried to haggle on the agreed price. (*Beat.*) You're one of the crude, the cruel, the nasty ones, the bargainers, the know-alls, the bloody-minded and you're ringing to say it won't ever happen again, you're a new woman, your life's changed.

---

* Pronounced like *pussy*. This word will be explained later.

(*It rings on.*)

Well, I don't believe you.

(*Phone stops.*)

No one ever changes.

(*She is waiting for the phone-call but is pretending to herself that she's come to work. She has designed a Spanish-style flamenco dress and is going to cut out the pattern she's drawn on her brown paper.*)

Change, Jessica? Let me tell you about change. Change is when white becomes black, a woman becomes a man, a Chinaman becomes an Englishman. But the insensitive do *not* become sensitive, the ugly do *not* become beautiful, and the foolish do *not* become wise. Believe me! An insurance agent may become a farmer after thirty years but that's not change, that's finding other parts of yourself.

(*The phone rings. She moves to it swiftly.*)

On the other hand you could be two and a half thousand pounds.

(*Answers in a foreign accent.*) 'Ello? Zee residence of Miss Samantha Milner. (*Pause.*) No, I am not she. I am zee cleaning lady and I assure you zis place needs very cleaning. 'Oo is zat, plise? (*Pause.*) Ah, Lady Madley. Well, she cannot see you zis evening because she is not 'ere. Even zee wicked must rest. (*Pause.*) No, no. A French proverb. (*Pause.*) Your son is what? (*Incredulous*) Getting engaged in two days' time? (*Laughing*) You want zat Samantha Milner make for you – ha! ha! – in two days – ha! ha! Yes, I tell 'er. I don't know what she say but I tell 'er. Excuse I laugh, I just woman who cleans but even zee peasant can dig a straight line. No, no. Obscure French proverb. *Merci! Au revoir!*

I know what she'll fucking say. She'll say go to Harrods or Paris or make it yourself. (*Pause.*) Better still, she'll say it'll cost a thousand more. Be exclusive! Right, Jessica? Hard to get! Right, Ninotchka? Make it difficult for them to buy you, that way you're appreciated, sought after, better paid.

(*Now that she is at her desk she catches sight of a pile of mail that seems to have been specially put aside. She picks up the top sheets.*)

Appeals, appeals, appeals! As if I didn't have *enough* to make me feel guilty.

(*She glances at the appeals one by one.*)

(*Reading*) The Samaritans . . . British Defence Aid Fund for Southern Africa . . . Friends of the Earth . . . 'Dear Miss Milner, you are one of a number of respected public figures we are asking to adopt a thousand trees in a Brazilian rainforest. I expect you are approached every day with a request to help a charity or to give to some worthy cause. Let me explain . . .'

(*She sits. Reaches for a cheque book.*)

No need to explain. I'll buy a thousand trees. Twenty-five pounds. There! So a few more wild flowers can survive. An exotic lizard or two.

(*Takes up bunch of papers again.*)

Celebrities Guild of Great Britain . . . tickets for the Gala dinner . . . awards to unsung heroes . . .

Tell me, Ninotchka, who is *not* an unsung hero?

Royal Society for Mentally Handicapped Children and Adults . . . Nightingale Home for the Jewish Aged . . . National Society for Epilepsy . . .

God help me, Jessica. Whose suffering do I choose first?

No blinding questions, Sam. We promised ourselves no blinding questions this evening.

That's not a real blinding question, Jessica, that's what's known in the business of living as a rhetorical question.

(*She writes a cheque.*)

There's a rumour you've got Jewish blood in your family, Sam. Twenty-five pounds. (*Pause.*) There's a blinding rumour that one day you'll grow old, Sam. Make it fifty.

(*From a desk drawer she pulls out a bottle of Jack Daniels whiskey. Pours herself a glass.*)

I think it's the inevitable letter I dread. 'My dear Samantha,' it will begin, 'you have made me realize I love my wife . . .'

I also love his wife! My good friend! What's that got to do with anything?!

I can remember how we first met. He gave a lecture. On women's clothes: 'The exposure of the mind by the concealment of the body!' How could I not go? Wasn't even his field. Historian of the Victorian years with a curiosity for clothes on the side. Dreadful organizers, dreadful hostess. I phoned. 'You are very bored,' I told him without introducing myself. 'Those people you are with are the killers of all time. I'm having a party. Come and join me. I'll put you right about women's clothes!' A dark voice from out the night! Adventure!

Nothing like that had ever happened to him. 'How will I know you?' he asked. 'You will know me,' I replied. (*Pause.*) He was so beautiful. (*Pause.*) And so married. (*Pause.*) And to such a wonderful woman. (*Pause.*) I fell in love with her, too.

(*Picks up sheaf of appeals.*)

Durham University Bolivia Expedition . . . International Fund for Animal Welfare . . . Nicaragua Health Fund . . . British Wildlife . . .

(*Reaching for cheque book, writing*) People should be healthy. Nicaragua Health Fund. Fifty pounds.

(*Warning*) This is going to be an expensive evening for you, Sam.

(*Turns on dummies.*) Which one of you said that? It's my money! All these noble people here looking up *Who's Who*, spending hours formulating the *best* letter to make me feel the *most* guilty? They should *know* they're succeeding, that someone out there *feels* guilty.

(*Returns to cutting out pattern.*)

You're talking to the dummies again, Sam. How many times must I tell you: talk to dummies you'll stop believing in your*self*.

Belief, Jessica? Let me tell you about belief. Belief is believing life is more important than belief. Belief is young and twenty and all the world loving you. Belief is every single person with a heart of gold, a head of brains, a sensitive soul, endless talents, the parts in harmony if only, if only, if only . . . (*Longingly*) Ah! if only . . .

When I was young I wrote in my diary, 'Dear God, I don't mind what happens to me as long as *something* does!'

(*Concentrates on cutting pattern.*)

He's full of ideas for making a fortune. Parts! 'Do you know the parts of things?' he asks. 'I know the parts of a garment,' I say. 'The underbodice back, the underbodice side front, the armhole facing – that kind of part?' 'Exactly!' he says. 'But do you know the parts of a car, a cathedral, a flower, clouds? You're at a shoot,' he says. 'This stunning model in your stunning creation, and your stunning setting is a stately home. "Stand her there," you say. "Where?" they ask. "By that part there," you say. "What part where?" they ask. "*That* part, the one with bits sticking out at the top . . ."' He's right! I don't know the name of the part of *any*thing! 'An Encyclopaedia of Parts,' he says. 'A fortune! Made for life!' He's always looking to be 'made for life'.

(*Cuts on in silence.*)

'My dear Samantha,' it will begin, 'you know you will always be someone special for me, but . . .'

I hate 'buts'. 'You're right, but . . .' 'It's a beautiful dress, but . . .' 'Normally I'd die for you, but . . .'

(*Cuts on in silence.*)

Do you enjoy being a mistress?

Who asked that? Which one of you brazen dummies asked that? Is that this evening's blinding question? 'Enjoy'? Let me tell you about 'enjoy'. 'Enjoy' is when you achieve what you set out to achieve, when you know what it is you *want* to achieve, when you have opinions, standards, a perspective on history, a cultural framework so that anywhere, any time, you know what the hell is being spoken about. 'Enjoy' is when your conscience is clear, you feel comfortable with yourself, you can look in a mirror and say 'good morning' instead of 'yeach'. When everything in you is good and sweet and innocent and the parts come together – I tell you! 'Enjoy' is when you love your*self* rather than your good friend's husband. I need another whiskey!

(*To the desk. The drawer. The bottle. The drink. Picks up sheaf of appeals.*)

'As you may be aware 1988 will be the 50th Anniversary of the *Anschluss* of Austria and the *Reichskristallnacht*, the night when the first vicious attacks were made on synagogues and Jewish property in Austria and Germany . . .'

Was I aware? I was not aware. Of how much else am I not aware? ~~Chile Solidarity Campaign . . . Save the Harvest in Tigray . . .~~

'Dear Miss Milner, we are writing to you about Irina Ratushinskaya. As you know she has recently been released from prison in Russia . . .'

(*Rises, to the dummies.*) OK, you choose. Money to help commemorate human suffering? Money for democracy? Money for food in Africa? Money for an individual victim of state oppression? And we haven't come to the end of the pile yet. A year's collection of unanswered appeals for help! They have to be faced.

(*Moves to rack of clothes.*)

What shall I wear for him tonight? Long, *décolleté*, clinging? Something sparkly with black net stockings, suspenders?

(Pulls a box of bottles towards her.)

And which perfume? Fiji? Aramis? Blazer by Anne Klein? Not really, they're for sport. Ralph Laurie? Tatiana? No, they're for day clothes. Eau de Floris by Nina Ricci? Mmm. Romantic but not sexy. Nocturnes by Caron? Paris by Yves St Laurent? Opium? I smell Opium on everyone. All day. Belongs to nightdresses actually. *(Beat.)* Don't laugh. He cares about such things. *(Beat.)* To be honest, so do I.

(Pause.)

I know, Jessica, he *promised* to phone but he may not be *able* to phone. He *may* be free or he may *not* be free. He *might* want to go to a theatre, a movie, a concert, a restaurant – or he might just want to *talk*.

(Pause.)

Or not.

(Pause.)

Make love.

(Pause.)

Or not.

(Pause.)

So, the dress to put stars in his eyes? The one to outline my lush curves? The stern, austere two-piece which if the truth be known really belongs to my middle age – with knee-length socks to remind him I was once a schoolgirl?

Oh, Jessica. Was I ever a schoolgirl? What did I think in those days? What did I feel, what did I imagine, what did I want for myself?

You notice she doesn't talk to *me* much, Jessica.

Well, you're such a fearsome woman, Ninotchka.

She's frightened I'll ask her a blinding question.

Ignore her, Sam. Tell us about being a young girl.

Go on, Babushka, tell us about the first time you seduced a young man.

A young boy, actually, when I was a young girl. About fifteen. I had always dreamed of seduction. The power that comes with it. Nothing brazen, nothing coy or coquettish. I hated all that in those days. But letting him know that you longed, that you ached, that with *you* there was the possibility – your eyes, your smile, a touch, a movement, a word – ah! the confidence then.

It was at a mixed camp for the children of Russian immigrants, in a river valley. I saw this boy, beautiful, intelligent, vivid, loved being alive – bit unworldly if the truth be known. And I found all that irresistible.

He'd attached himself to another girl. Sweet and matronly. 'Wrong,' I said to myself. 'She doesn't see you,' I said to myself. 'I'm what you need, and *you*', I said to myself, 'are what I will have.' And on the last night, when he was about to capture the embrace he'd worked so hard to achieve, she fell asleep. As matronly girls often do. And I reached out a hand which I knew he'd take and I laid it on my firm, young breast, and O how that nipple rose and carried his heat to my audacious parts. While he worked for a mere matronly kiss I had worked my alchemy to lose him deep inside me. Mmm!

Don't get me wrong, Jessica, we were equals.

Only some of us, as has been recorded, are more equals than others, are we not, Babushka?

(*Looks again at the four previous letters of appeal. Reaches for cheque book.*)

The individual starting a new life after prison, I think. (*Writing*) Irina Ratushinskaya Fund, fifty pounds.

What a good safety valve. Do you think they know this, the charity-mongers? 'Let's write to Samantha Milner, unmarried, no children, she must be stealing *some*body's husband – loaded with guilts!' They're a bit like the police, the charity-mongers, they know we've all got something to hide.

(*Returns to cutting. Takes the Jack Daniels with her.*)

This won't pay the bills. You have a job to do, Sam.

(*Cuts on in silence.*)

You don't really have a job to do. You have a staff of six. You're just killing time, waiting.

(*Cuts on in silence.*)

I can remember my *first* married lover. We made a pact. '*I* won't tell you about my other lovers and you won't tell me how much you really love your wife and children.'

(*Cuts on in silence.*)

But the second one – he was mean. Came for a week and brought his own shampoo. I waited to see if he'd take the half-finished bottles away with him. He did! Also a half-finished bottle of wine. Which finished us!

(*Pause.*)

Then there was the one who cried when it was done.

(*Pause.*)

And the one who picked a quarrel five minutes after.

(*Pause.*)

And the one who immediately phoned his wife to see how she was.

(*Pause.*)

Do you think that perhaps you don't really *like* men, Babushka?

Is that your idea of a 'blinding question', Ninotchka? Well, I think it's a stupid question and I have no time for stupid questions. I have this gorgeous flamenco dress to cut.

(*Cuts on in silence.*)

'My dear Samantha,' it will begin, 'I suppose you knew this letter would come one day . . .'

(*Pours herself another drink. Although it began as playfulness,* SAM, *the more drunk she becomes, assumes the characters she has given to her dummies. From here on there are three characters.*)

NINOTCHKA: Are you an honest woman, Babushka?

JESSICA: Leave her alone, Ninotchka. Have pity on a working girl.

SAMANTHA: I'm crippled with honesty. Problem with honesty is that it inspires an excess of self-criticism which doesn't always apply.

NINOTCHKA: Come now, Babushka, you *think* you're honest. But what about all those dark corners of the soul, those hidden recesses of the mind, those delicious secrets of the heart.

JESSICA: You're a spiteful old hag, Ninotchka, you know that?

SAMANTHA: Thank you, Jessica. You I could always rely on to understand.

NINOTCHKA: But the question, Babushka, the one really blinding question you dare not face.

SAMANTHA: *What* question? There are no questions I can't face. My friends *love* me at their parties because of the questions I ask and the questions I answer.

NINOTCHKA: All of them?

SAMANTHA: *All* of them!

NINOTCHKA: She's not being honest now, is she, Jessica?

JESSICA: Ninotchka, you're overstepping the mark.

SAMANTHA: Thank you, Jessica.

(*Pause.*)

NINOTCHKA: *You* think the wife should feel *proud*, don't you, Babushka? Proud that no mistress has been good enough to take him away from her, proud that she's not married to a timid, faithful, spineless wimp but to a man who dares and is dazzling. Which is a reflection of her. (*Beat.*) Only one thing wrong with that, isn't there, Babushka? The wife's become your good friend.

JESSICA: Then why him, Sam? Your good friend's husband? Why him?

SAMANTHA: (*Desperately*) Because, Jessica, he doesn't compete with me! He's the most balanced man I know. He listens, he explains, he asks questions, he can change his mind. I feel safe with him, looked after, special in his life. He has a still centre and – and – Oh, be honest, Sam (*changing to growls and humour*) – the sex is lascivious and breathtaking!

NINOTCHKA: She makes it sound so virtuous. Let me tell you about virtue, Jessica, and the ease with which one lies, feeling no guilt whatsoever. Let me tell you about virtue and the ease with which one is devious and expects virtue from others. Let me tell you about the virtuous heart that can harden while the rest remains soft, sweet and tender – because let there be no misunderstanding, Babushka is all these things – a fine and lovely and virtuous person, except in this one respect: she lies to her good friend with the talent of a sublime actress. Her good friend whom she loves and, let there be no misunderstanding about that either, her good friend can ask her life of her! But – when she has her good friend's husband in her arms, on her lips and between those ample, fleshy thighs, her good friend is banished from her thoughts. They do not exist for each other. Now, ask her how. How, Sam, how can this be?

(*Pause.*)

She won't answer? Then I'll tell you how this can be, my dear sister. Because real joy, real happiness, the joy and happiness that love brings is not only fleeting, it's rare. You may never be given another chance. Virtue, betrayal, loyalty, guilt, all pale, fade, are as nothing to that ecstasy which may never come again. Imagine! To live only once and never, never taste that ecstasy! Imagine!

(*She returns to her cutting. One of the sheets arrests her attention.*)

SAMANTHA: This is not going to work. Did I draw this? Couldn't have been concentrating.

(*She attempts to redraw the outlines.*)

My daddy wanted me to be an academic. A thinker! Wanted me to add at least one original thought to the world. But I didn't have an original thought. Not even one. 'I want to be a dress designer, Daddy,' I said. 'I want to make women look beautiful!' 'Cursi!' he yelled at me. 'Beauty comes from what people *are*, not what they wear. Cursi! Cursi! Cursi!' 'What', I asked him, 'does "cursi" mean?' And he told me a story.

In Venezuela there lived a bourgeois family by the name of Sicur. They had three daughters who were very arrogant and pretentious, and said things like, 'Oh, look at the moon, how it moves my soul.' And, 'I love music, it makes me weep.' And, 'When I have a baby it will be the pride of my life.'

Nearly everyone was impressed by the girls and they were invited to parties where all the other young women tried to be like them and invent things to say which could be accompanied by a meaningful sigh. One evening, at just such a party, a young woman was heard to say in a loud voice, 'Oh, how mysterious the nights are.' At which a young man, who hated the Sicur girls, cried out so that they heard, 'Oh my God, another cursi!' The word stuck. Cur–si, Si–cur, cursi! Kitsch of the heart! And my father, who himself wanted to add an original thought to the world but failed, warned me in life against many kinds of cursi. 'Beware', he said, 'of cursi of the heart, the hearth, and the intellect.'

I brought home a young man once, from art college. 'This is my father,' I introduced them. 'Daddy, this is James. He's studying sculpture.' My father didn't like him. His eyes, they kept moving. 'I hope there's no nonsense going on between you.' He always came quickly to the point, my father. James was incredulous. 'I believe in sexual friendships,' said James with hard skin on his hands. 'Cursi of the *heart*!' exploded my father.

He hated people who said such things as, 'There's nothing like a fire to make a room feel homely!' '*Domestic* cursi!' screamed my father.

He despised those who defended religious dogma with facile arguments. 'But can you prove there *isn't* a God? Can you prove there *isn't* a life after this one?' '*Intellectual* cursi!' cried my father. Cursi! Cursi! Cursi!

(*Long pause.*)

'My dear Samantha,' it will begin, 'there is a corner of my heart that will forever be . . .'

(*Pause.*)

NINOTCHKA: Well, Jessica, you notice she didn't ever answer that question about not really liking men at all.

(*Moves down to her desk.*)

SAMANTHA: Stop this, Sam. Madness! You're letting two dummies rule your life.

(*Pours herself a drink. Picks up sheaf of appeals.*)

Colombian Volcano Appeal . . . Gay Sweatshop Theatre Company . . . Campaign Against Censorship . . . Marie Curie Memorial Foundation . . . Survival International . . . for the rights of threatened tribal people . . .

(*Pause.*)

If only I believed in God, everything would be easier. Confessors, explanations, certitudes, a moral centre that held the parts . . .

NINOTCHKA: Well, none of *us* is going to paradise, that's for sure. Purgatory for us. The halfway house. Where each of us is going to be given the one task we loathe most on earth. You hate ironing? You'll be made to iron. You hate scrubbing floors? You'll be made to scrub floors. You hate washing up? You'll be made to wash up. Especially pots of burnt meat.

JESSICA: Have more sympathy for her, Ninotchka.

NINOTCHKA: (*Viciously*) Why?

JESSICA: She's *your* bread and butter too, you know.

NINOTCHKA: 'Not by bread alone!'

JESSICA: Oh, you're full of such cursi cant, Ninotchka.

NINOTCHKA: Very good, Jessica. Cursi cant! Witty! Yes. I like that. Cursi cant!

(*Pause.*)

SAMANTHA: 'My dear Samantha,' it will begin, 'I cannot live any longer with the guilt . . .'

Stop this! Stop it, stop it! Haven't you heard? There is a curse upon the land. The best men have been turned to stone. There is a dearth of poets. You'll never find another like him. Get on your knees.

NINOTCHKA: Oh my! How apocalyptically she speaks. But how easy it is for such as you to grab the poets, Babushka. Glamorous career, energy, friends, a large Slavic family of brothers, sisters, cousins, uncles, aunts. You live in this glorious city of political activity and intellectual stimulation and a dozen arts and a thousand and one culinary delights. But what about the poor provincial woman whose mind is large and whose husband is dull? The lonely country wife whose passion is stormy but whose horizons are hedges? The suburban wife who discovered literature at a suburban school and finds her transformed suburban imagination falling on stony suburban ground? What advice do you have for them? The wife who's made a mistake? The middle-aged spinster who can see it all passing by? The desperate widows? The sixty-year-olds who as we all know are dormant volcanoes? You who have rationalized your treachery, what advice do you have for them?

SAMANTHA: Well, well, Ninotchka. Is that your blinding question? Based on cheap guilt? You want me to respond to other people's mistakes when here I'm confronted with *real* misfortune – misery perpetrated by man and nature? You'll have to do better than that, Ninotchka darling.

(*Pulls cheque book towards her.*)

Survival International, I think. For the rights of threatened tribal people. Seventy-five pounds.

(*Another drawer. A box of chocolates, picks one and eats.*)

The great Russian dancer Pavlova said, 'Artists should know all about love and learn to live without it.'

(*Returns with box of chocolates to her cutting.*)

And then there was the lover who sang given any pretext. He'd see a shop called Daisy's and he'd say, 'Oh look, a shop called Daisy's!' (*Sings*) 'Daisy, Daisy, give me your answer, do . . .' Or I'd tell him about a difficult client and I'd say, 'I can't wait to get her out of my hair.' (*Sings*) 'I'm gonna wash that man right out of my hair, I'm gonna wash that man right out of my hair . . .'

(*Pause. Picks another chocolate.*)

Once we passed an ecclesiastical bookshop in New York called The Hallelujah Bookstore. 'DON'T,' I said.

(*Tantalizing pause. The 'girls' wait.*)

JESSICA: And did he, Sam, did he?

SAMANTHA: (*Arms in the air, with gusto, sings*) 'HA–LLELUJAH! HA–LLELUJAH! Hallelujah! Hallelujah! Ha – le – ey – lu – jah!' I have had them all.

(*She makes her final cuts. A skirt needs ironing. Switches on iron. Waits.*)

NINOTCHKA: Notice once more, sister, the artful way Babushka has avoided the question? Like all these letters of appeal which she kept putting aside. But there's one blinding question waiting, isn't there, Babushka? One you can't avoid any more than you can avoid the world's cries or the cries of –

SAMANTHA: Phone! Phone! Why isn't it time for him to phone? A chocolate. I need a chocolate or two. Let me see now. Which one shall we have next? Burnt sugar crunch in truffle? Roast almonds in cream? Soft toffee between biscuit? Oh look, a Jack Daniels liqueur.

(*Bites. Breathes deeply. Returns to ironing.*)

There was one lover I met at a dinner party who was very reluctant to begin a conversation. He seemed – I can't describe it any other way – to flinch from it, as though knowing that inevitably the question would come: what do *you* do for a living? 'Oh, nothing interesting,' he said. I pressed. 'Not as interesting as *your* profession,' he resisted. He'd obviously devised many ways of trying to fend off the reply. 'Come,' I said, 'it must be or you wouldn't be at this table.' 'I'm in manufacture,' he said at last. I waited. 'Some people', I said, 'would be satisfied with that reply. Not me, I'm afraid. What *kind* of manufacture?' I am as you know relentless. He capitulated. 'Toilet paper,' he replied.

Well, I understood. It *was* very difficult to know what to say after that. And I could see him watching me, closely, as though he judged people by the way they responded. It was unnerving. Some, I suppose, would exaggerate their interest. 'Toilet paper? Oh, *really*?' Some probably splutter all over the place. 'Toilet paper? Ah – oh – mmm – yeeees – weeeelllll . . .' Most people probably change the subject as soon as they can. 'Toilet paper? And do you have children?'

Me, I was to the point. Tough old Sam. 'Toilet paper?' I said. 'And is there much competition?' You should have seen his little face light up. 'As a matter of fact,' he said, 'there is. From Korea. They make it much more cheaply than we can!' 'Ah,' I asked, quick as a lizard, 'but is it as good?' 'Oh no,' he cried, and we spent another half-hour on the technical problems involved in the manufacture of that without which life can be complicated, and the rest of the evening on the counter-productiveness of terrorism, on music, literature, love, sexual politics, his place or my place and many other things without which life would be complicated.

(*Irons in silence.*)

NINOTCHKA: And babies?

(*Irons in silence.*)

And babies?

(*Irons in silence.*)

And babies?

SAMANTHA: You are relentless!

(*Moves down for another Jack Daniels.*)

OK. You want to know about babies? Let me tell you about babies. I don't relate to them. I don't understand why they're not adults. I don't understand why they're there, crying, smelling, demanding, helpless. I get paralysed confronted with such helplessness. They need twenty-four-hour watching and they've got no conversation.

NINOTCHKA: Liar!

SAMANTHA: I just am not at one with the children of this world. They make me feel childish!

NINOTCHKA: Liar!

SAMANTHA: And this is not the world I want to bring them into.

NINOTCHKA: Liar.

SAMANTHA: Your whole life has to revolve round them. I'm too busy, too young, too selfish.

NINOTCHKA: Liar! Liar!

SAMANTHA: All right! I want my body firm, I want it to stay the way it is. I can't bear pain, change, disappointment, all that loving, all that doting, all that dependence, giving, giving, giving! What can I do? I'm just not maternal. Some people are born tone-deaf, dyslexic, brain-damaged, they have deficiencies, allergies. I once had a client who was allergic to herself! What can I do? I don't have the imagination to comprehend what it's like to be a child and not to be an adult. Jesus Christ! I came up here to work, not to be stretched on the rack by the Inquisition. Why am I letting this woman upset me, Jessica? And why isn't it time for the phone to ring?

NINOTCHKA: (*A frenzy*) And will you destroy for him? And will you betray who you are for him? And will you offend what you value for him? And cripple and mock and pollute and spit upon all that you love for him?

SAMANTHA: Who is she, this Ninotchka? Who? Who? Some mad woman that's who!

(*Silence.*)

(*Exhausted, on the verge of tears*) I am so tired of myself, Jessica. I can cross my legs with a flash of thigh before modestly pulling down my skirt. I can swing my hips, sparkle my eyes, smile secret smiles of promise. I can feign world-weariness, prick intellects, be wicked and witty and spuriously wise and it all comes to me with such ease and I am very, very tired of it.

Oh, I ache to be young again. I miss, I miss, I so miss my days of blood and youth.

NINOTCHKA: Cursi, Babushka, cursi, cursi, cursi!

SAMANTHA: *Not* cursi. Pain is not cursi.

NINOTCHKA: But nostalgia is.

JESSICA: Oh shut up, Ninotchka. Can't you see the woman's upset? What do you think a psychiatrist would get out of her if not nostalgia? Talk, Samantha, tell us about your youth.

NINOTCHKA: Especially the 'blood' part.

JESSICA: Ignore her, Sam. She's an acerbic old hag. We've all got one of those for a friend. Come. Youth. Parents. Mother and father. Start with them.

(*Long pause. Now we really witness a tortured soul wrestling with itself.*)

SAMANTHA: They had a great capacity for joy.

NINOTCHKA: You realize power goes from you to him, Babushka?

SAMANTHA: They could dance to disco music in the middle of the day.

NINOTCHKA: Balanced, you say? Subtle? But *he* still sets the ground rules, Babushka.

74

SAMANTHA: Come the spring they'd rush out each morning to see which were the first flowers breaking through.

NINOTCHKA: You can't confide in anyone, can't share distress with anyone.

SAMANTHA: They delighted in their children, their grandchildren, in company, good food, good wine, other people's success.

NINOTCHKA: And the odd night is *never* enough, is it? Or the rare weekend?

SAMANTHA: Oh, they were not without angers, frailties, flaws but – I don't know. One felt happier when they were around, reassured. They had a still centre. The parts held.

NINOTCHKA: And there's no equality there, Babushka, no give and take.

SAMANTHA: It was their nature to be happy as the nature of some was to be joyless: to be generous as others were mean, to be sunny as others were sour.

NINOTCHKA: Face it, Babushka. This affair has no future and it's demeaning and lonely.

SAMANTHA: They radiated. We basked in it. Stretched our limbs and depended upon it.

NINOTCHKA: And you still haven't answered the one, big, blinding question, have you . . . ?

SAMANTHA: And they attracted hatred and they attracted devotion and we adored them and I miss them, I miss them, I miss them.

NINOTCHKA: . . . Sam, Sam, Babushka, Sam?

(*She now speaks very fast as though to drown out the other voice.*)

SAMANTHA: And he has all these weird and wonderful ideas for making a fortune. To be made for life! Always looking to be made for life. He wants to become an agent for renting out farmland to African states which suffer from drought. He wants to write a history of those revolutions which massacre their thinkers and burn their books. He has this idea for a new diet of citrus fruits and honey in the morning and yoghurt and honey in the evening. And it's very good. I've tried it. But I'll never be any good at diets, I'm too curious to be disciplined or moral about anything!

(*Abrupt halt. Moves to her desk. Another whiskey. She looks at her sheaf of appeals.*)

The National Jazz Centre, a fund-raising concert . . . Parliamentary Wives for the Release of Soviet Jewry . . . Mineworkers Defence Committee . . . 'Dear Miss Milner . . . our productions will integrate the different parts of performance disciplines . . . dance, movement, mime, acting . . . our first production . . . *Petrushka* . . . in the piazza of Covent Garden . . .'

(*Reaches for her cheque book.*)

Most people are giving money to the miners, and parliamentary wives know everyone who's important. *No* one is supporting jazz or the arts . . . (*Writing*) Project Petrushka . . . one hundred pounds . . . National Jazz Centre . . . one hundred pounds . . .

NINOTCHKA: I think guilts are cursi, Babushka. Cursyonomy of the heart. There! I've coined a new word. Cursyonomy. Cursyonomous. Cursionic. Cursyisms. Throw everything at them – old age, physical handicap, starvation! Give them no rest! Afflicted children, cultural neglect, plundering capitalists! Agitate them! Distress them! Interfere with their happiness! Maimed animals, oppression, deprivation, disease, disaster! Cursi! Cursi! Cursi, cursi, cursi!

(*Swiftly to iron.*)

SAMANTHA: The phone's out of order! He's had an accident! His wife's had an accident! One of his children! God in heaven, it's time! Ring, damn you! Rescue me. I – NEED – RESCUING!

(*Irons in silence.*)

'If we are honest,' it will begin, 'all things must end . . .'

NINOTCHKA: And what will you do then, Babushka? Rage? Let me tell you about rage. Like a wife, you'll rage. You could justify his betrayal for *you*. (*Mock ardour*) 'How can you deny such a grand passion? Where is your courage, adventure, your manhood? Can't you see that to love me is the supreme test, the risk of thrilling risks . . . ?' Oh yes, Babushka, you had the language to taunt, inflame and justify your 'man with the still centre', but for *him* to leave *you*? For *him* to betray *you*? You have hell in you ready for that, have you not, Babushka? Oh, have you not! Queen of the double standard! That's you! Of the double standard, Queen!

SAMANTHA: Stop her, Jessica, stop her or I'll do something drastic.

NINOTCHKA: And the question, Babushka, the one big blinding

question? Are you ready for it? All that lovely honesty set up to receive it? Think you've given enough away to charity?

JESSICA: Too far, Ninotchka, too far! You don't really care about honesty, do you? All you care about is pain. You're jealous, aren't you? You don't think she deserves what she's achieved, do you? It's not fair to be endowed with beauty *and* talent *and* good fortune *and* a lovely loving lover. What a mean and tawdry little tart you are, Ninotchka. What an ungenerous tight-arsed sanctimonious vixen, a killer, a sadistic despot, a –

NINOTCHKA: Ask her! Ask her! Let's have none of your pious mercy, Jessica. No lachrymosity this night, my friend. This night is judgment night. Ask her: How can she *love* a man who betrays his wife? Ask her that!

(*She puts her hand on the hot iron.*)

SAMANTHA: Get her out of my head, pleeeeeese! (*Hand off.*) Pho–o–o–o–ne me!

(*She moves quickly to a first-aid cupboard. Takes out a tube for burns.*)

JESSICA: You've been drinking too much, Sam.

SAMANTHA: I know I have, Jessica, I know it.

JESSICA: Stop working, stop drinking, stop talking to yourself and sit down.

SAMANTHA: Yes, Jessica, I will, I will. I'll do all that.

JESSICA: You can have a chocolate or two but not the liqueurs.

(SAMANTHA *moves down to the box of chocolates.*)

I don't know why you've worked yourself up into such a state tonight, Sam. Why tonight of all nights? Wherefore is this night different from all other nights?

(*She picks up sheaf of appeals.*)

(*Lights go down very, very slowly.*)

SAMANTHA: Amnesty International . . . Jews Against Apartheid . . . Christian Aid . . . 'Dear Samantha Milner, to you the suffering in Africa may seem never ending. Horrors that cry out for help. Your help. And sometimes you almost wish you could forget. Until . . .'

(*Blackout.*)

ANNIE WOBBLER

Annie Wobbler was first broadcast in German by Suddeutscher Rund-funk on 3 February 1983, under the title *Annie, Anna, Annabella*. The English-language premiere took place on 5 July 1983 at the Birmingham Repertory Theatre Studio, with Nichola McAuliffe, directed by the author and designed by Pamela Howard. This production subsequently transferred to the New End Theatre, London, on 26 July 1983 and was revived on 13 November 1984 at the Fortune Theatre, London. The New York opening was on 16 October 1986 at the Westbeth Theater Center with Sloane Bosniak, directed by Gerald Chapman.

Annie Wobbler was conceived to be performed without an interval. During the run in Birmingham I became anxious about the audience's ability to concentrate for 85 minutes non-stop, so I asked Nichola to give one performance with an interval. She was reluctant but agreed. She hated the break. I questioned members of the audience. All said they didn't want or need an interval. It broke their concentration. I believe greater impact is achieved, and of course the actress is challenged to present a *tour de force*, if there is no break and the action is continuous. I have laid out the text here (pp. 97–8) to show how it must be done if an interval is insisted upon.

A.W.

Annie Wobbler was originally written for the talents of my friend Nichola McAuliffe.

A.W.

Part One

ANNIE WOBBLER

Music: 'Ah, Sweet Mystery of Life'. *

Part of a two-roomed tenement attic flat. Stone steps lead up to the landing outside. The landing serves as the kitchen where there is a gas stove; an old wire-meshed kitchen cabinet with a drop leaf which acts as a table; a deal stool. At the foot of the steps, in a corner, is a sink with only a cold-water tap.

ANNIE WOBBLER, part-time tramp, part-time cleaning woman, is finishing scrubbing the 'kitchen'. Her actions are meticulous. She must once have been a maid in an upper-class household, her speech and manner carry the echoes of 're-fainment'. Years of decline have made her eccentric. She wears a number of voluminous skirts which hide all manner of things. The hat on her head seems ever to have been there. Everything she wears is black with odd touches of green.

ANNIE speaks to 'madam' offstage right who is not there, and to 'God' (or her alter ego) who seems ever to be in a crevice of the far ceiling above the heads of the audience. Note: important that the actress identifies which lines are addressed to whom. She speaks sternly, as though always telling someone off – the habit of defending her eccentricity from mocking children, perhaps; and in between what we can hear she mumbles. She seems never able to be still, bringing articles out of her skirt to check and exchange for others in her 'old woman's bundle'.

These are the movements of her scrubbing: rag into pail, slop water around area to be cleaned. Rub huge Lifebuoy soap on to huge scrubbing brush. Scrub! Wring out rag, make a length, draw length down bit by bit to gather soapy area, squeeze out, draw length down again, and so on. Final dry-up with wrung cloth. She enjoys the actions. The ritual satisfies her.

When done she pours dirty water down sink, fills it with fresh, places it on stove, small light.

Spring 1939.

* Richard Crooks sings 'Ah, Sweet Mystery of Life' from *Naughty Marietta*, by Young and Herbert, with orchestra, available from BBC archives.

ANNIE *

They tell me I smell. I don't smell nothing, madam. But then no one don't know anything about themselves, do they? Lessun they look in a mirror. (*Idea.*) I'll look in one, shall I? Got one here, somewhere.

(*Rummages among her numerous skirts, withdraws a chipped hand-bag mirror.*)

Long time since I looked in a mirror. Don't tell you much, 'cept you're growing old. That's all I see. I see this face but I don't know anything about it, 'cept it's growing old. (*Finds it. Raises it to her face.*) 'Mornin', Annie Wobbler,' I say. 'Mornin'.' Me talking to myself, that is. 'You're growing old, Annie Wobbler,' I say. 'Old! old!' Funny feeling looking at yourself and not knowing what you see. So I don't do it much. Old! What did I do to deserve that? Don't understand nothing, me. (*Pause.*) I don't smell. (*Sniffs.*) I mean that's not a smell, that's me, madam.

(*Puts away mirror, lowers leaf of kitchen cabinet. She rummages among her skirts and finds tin plate, tin mug, knife to place on table. Talks meanwhile.*)

She's very polite about it though, the madam. She only ses, 'You washed today, Annie?' I ses, 'Course I did, madam, course I did.' I don't know what she takes me for.

They're Jew people. (*To God*) Your lot! They don't do no Jew things like I've seen other Jew people do, candles and prayers and straps round their arms, but they're Jew people all the same. Like I don't do no Christian things but I'm a Christian person all the same.

(*Takes knife to stone steps, sharpens it.*)

No, I don't do no Christian things. I'm a sinner, madam. You're a sinner, Annie Wobbler, your mother would be ashamed of you, so it's thank-your-lucky-stars she's dead and gone, thank them! There! Now look what you've gone and done. Made yourself cry, you stupid girl. Dumb! (*Pause. Instant recovery.*) 'Bout time I had my tea, I think.

(*She pours milk into cup, lifts tea from tea caddy into tea strainer, in preparation. Her alter ego seems to be telling her she's put too much in. She retrieves a little back in the caddy.*)

---

* In Part One I have indicated Cockney dialect only here and there by dropping odd 'h'. It would have made tiresome reading to have carried it throughout. But ANNIE is certainly a Cockney.

Wonder what's in the cabinet. Madam said I could help myself. You're very kind, madam. 'I trust you, Annie,' she said. 'We don't have anything, besides.' (*Opens it.*) She's right! (*Taking them out*) A little cheese, a little butter, some Jew-bread. They don't have much more'n what I've got. Lord knows how you can afford sixpence for a cleaning woman like me, madam. They can't.

(*She butters, then cuts loaf, holding bread to her bosom and sawing towards herself.*)

She tell me, 'We'll give you sixpence or some bread and tea. Whichever's around!' Fair enough. Scrub a couple of floors, flight of steps. Fair enough.

What's this? Rollmops? I like rollmops. Madam ses they're pickled herrings. (*Calling out*) Pickled herrings to you, madam, rollmops to us! (*Opens jar, forks out one.*) You're very kind, madam. (*Bites.*) Funny people, foreigners.

(*She sits to her bread and butter. Folds slice, pulls out soft centre, stuffs crust in pocket.*)

For the birds. (*Beat.*) Still, that's what comes of living in the East End. All sorts live here. You'd think because all sorts live here they'd leave you alone. But they don't, madam, they don't.

(*The kettle is boiling. She makes her mug of tea by pouring water over the tea she's prepared in the strainer.*)

Not the way I was taught to make tea. Never use twice-boiled water, my first madam said, you boil the goodness away. Fresh water, heat the pot, a spoonful for each person, one for 'is knob, and then leave. Not like this. (*Mug cupped in hands, she sips.*) Funny people, foreigners. (*Sips and eats.*) You're very kind, madam.

I mean if I walked around Knightsbridge where I *used* to work, I'd understand. What's a girl like this doing up Knightsbridge, my other madam would ask, for sure. But not here, not in the East End. Everyone's common here, madam, why should they stop *me*?

(*Imitating policeman*) 'Where you off to then?'

'I'm off to do some work so leave me be.'

'You? Work? What work? Who for?'

'Cleaning for a respectable madam that's who for so you mind your business and I'll mind mine.' That upset him.

'You can't talk to me like that, missus. I'm an officer of the law and I've a right to stop and question who I please.'

He was young so I forgive him, though why I should I don't know because the young is supposed to respect the old not that the old respect the young or the old respect the old or anybody any more respects anybody.

'What's your name?'

'Annie Wobbler!' I ses it defiant-like. 'Annie Wobbler!'

'Annie who?'

'Wobbler! Wobbler, Wobbler, Wobbler!' I get very angry when people make fun of my name, even before they start to make fun I get angry.

'Where d'you get a name like that from?' he asks.

'I had a mother, didn't I, and a father? A good woman and a good man with a good name.'

'Funny name!' he ses.

'Oh?' I ses. 'Funny?'

'Wobbler,' he ses. And he wobbles. Like they all do.

And you're supposed to laugh. They do, I don't!

'Funny names?' I tell 'im. 'I'll give you funny names. Mister Katz who doesn't like dogs! Mrs Smelley who washes too much! Miss Bubbles what burst! Mister Horse, and Hearse, and Lamb, and Sod, and Mrs Sore-at-heart, and Mister D'Eath-at-your-door, and Mister Paine-in-the-arse!' That shut him up a bit. 'Funny names?' I tell 'im. 'I'll give you funny names!'

(*She rises to wash mug and plate in sink.*)

Then he asks about my father. 'What's that to you?' I tell 'im.

'You interest me,' he ses.

'Oh I do, do I?'

My father! I don't remember what my father did. What did he want to go and ask me that for, madam? 'You've no right to ask me about my parents, that's no business of yours and not in your call of duty. My name's Annie Wobbler, I sleep in Rowton House and I work for my living doing for people. Now 'op it!'

(*Dries with tea cloth hanging on side of cabinet.*)

Who can remember? I think my father was a Frenchy, father, sisters, brothers. I had them all. Dead and gone. 'Cept this sister. Now *she* had money. Don't know where from. Used to think some of it should've come my way. She never helped me is all I know. She tell me . . . she tell me the money . . . she tell me that the money . . .

Now what did she tell me! (*Pause. Her memory protects itself. Angrily*) Oh, I don't know what she tell me! (*Pause.*) But she 'ad a baby so I couldn't stay with 'er. A bright little youngster *he* was, madam. Always said his prayers. But *she* weren't no good. 'Annie,' she ses to me, 'you can 'ave something to eat and then you must go.' Well, madam . . .

> (*Tucks mug, plate and knife back into folds of her skirt. Reaches for her bundle, sits on stool, opens bundle, sets aside old black shoes, brush and black polish; places two old tins on drop leaf. One she rattles, it has buttons in them. The other she opens, it has tobacco. From a pocket she draws out cigarette ends she's picked off the street. Throughout remaining passages she will polish her 'best' over-polished shoes, and unpick cigarette ends to fill her tobacco tin.*)

Not even photos left. Just faces. I see them. Who knows, my father might even have been one of you Jew people. So, one God's as good as another I say, and I go to synagogue on Saturdays and church on Sundays. Take no risks! (*Beat.*) You need a family.

Family. What'd he want to go and ask me that for? Questions! Everybody asks questions. They all want to know about you. Madam ses, 'Annie,' she ses, 'Annie, how did you get like this?' What a question! (*Considers it. Gloom.*)

Because I was a nothing, madam, and I knowed I was a nothing. That's knowledge for you. I wasn't told, I wasn't treated bad, but it come to me. Nothing! A nothing Annie Wobbler! Nothing brains and nothing looks and nothing grace. A serving-maid-for-other-people! A bag of rags and bones. Sack of old coal, that was me. (*Calling*) Sack o'coal! Sack o'coal! They used to come on lorries, one man driving, one heavin' an' callin'. Sack o'coal! Got all the parts wrong when they put me together. Needed to rub me out and draw me again. (*Pause. Remembering*) Sack o'coal! (*Beat.*) We was all young once, madam.

(*Abruptly changing mood*) The first people I ever worked for was real good to me they was. Down in Surrey. Forget the name of the village, madam, but it *was* Surrey. Pretty. And a pretty house. There was five bedrooms upstairs, a drawing room downstairs, and a dining room, and a library cos they was very high-class and they read a lot. And naturally a kitchen. A large kitchen with a whopping Aga cooker, and lots of brass pots on the walls. But the rest of the house was modern, all modern. The kitchen was old-fashioned but everywhere else was full of newfangled things. That's what the madam was like. She'd no sooner see something in town she'd go on at the master begging and pleading and giving him a dozen and one reasons why they should have it. And they usually did. Very rich they were. But sweet, and good-natured, always a kind word for the servants, and sometimes a penny slipped in your hand. And young. The madam was young. I used to look at her and say, 'You're very young to be a madam of a big house like this.' And that used to make her laugh. 'I'm not a madam,' she'd say. 'A madam isn't always a nice person. You *call* me madam but I'm *mistress* of the house,' she say, and I didn't understand what she was on about. 'You're the madam to me so I call you madam,' I tell 'er, and that was that. (*Pause.*) Young. Both of us. Her and me. And beautiful. I used to stare at her. Blue eyes she had, I remember, and milky hair and creamy skin. Noble. She liked me staring at her, I could tell. Always pretended she didn't know, but I knew she knew. Got to her when I was seventeen and stayed eighteen months. Reckon I must've loved her. Young. Both of us.

(*Abruptly changing mood*) What did I leave for if they was so kind? I can't remember, madam. I just felt – I don't know – I just felt I had to leave. Go somewhere else. There were lots of places down in Surrey, and the madam gave me a good reference. A very good reference as a matter of fact. Look. I got it here, somewhere.

(*She stands, turns her back to audience secretively, rummages in her skirts, takes out a bundle of letters, old, tied up with clumsy string.*)

Look. All references. Kept them all. Cos y'see I couldn't ever stay in one place. I'd work a year, eighteen months and then had to move. Don't ask me why, madam. I don't know why. I never knew why.

(*She's finished untying letters. Looks through them.*)

Here it is. The first reference I ever got. Cor! I haven't looked at this for years, not for years.

(*She extracts first reference, looks at it in silence as though reading it. Then –*)

I never could read. Nor write. Nor add. Nor dance. Nor talk proper. The master once tried to teach me to ride a bicycle but I never found the way to balance, and I hurt myself so many times I got frightened and give up. (*Returns to letter.*) But I *remember* what it said cos there was another girl what read it to me again and again so I learned it. (*Pause. Remembering*) This other girl! Cor! I'd forgotten her.

Now *she* got on. *She* had a strong nature. Tiny but – ooooh, fierce! No bigger'n this she was, with green eyes and red hair and energy like a steam engine. I used to watch her and get tired. Now here, listen to this, madam. She not only did all she was told, but she invented things what needed to be done. Bloody went around looking for them! Well, I wasn't going to do that! I did what I was told, but if no one told, I didn't do it! Not old redhead though. You looked at her and you knew, she was alive every minute of the day. Not like me, madam. Most of the day I'm dead. I'm dead or not there. Don't know where I go because when I come back I can't think where I've been. But the red-headed steam engine, she was filled every second with thinking or asking or doing or planning. Whew! *She* weren't made for service. '*You* aren't made for service,' I told her. 'No one's made for service,' she say, 'but you do have to start somewhere, don't you?' She started, I didn't! Got all the parts wrong when they put me together. Needed to rub me out and draw again.

(*Finally getting to letter*) 'To whomever it may concern.' I used to love saying that to myself. 'To whomever it may concern. Annie Wobbler is a good and willing girl. She is completely trustworthy and will work for anyone who is kind to her.' Ha! All I did was tell the madam when the soap had gone small, and when the toilet paper was needed. 'To whomever it may concern.'

Had to leave, though, madam. Always felt full of holes and had to leave. They left bits out when they put me together, see, I couldn't never understand nothing, madam. All a foreign language to me. Nothing! A nothing Annie Wobbler. (*Calling*) Sack o'coal! Sack o'coal! (*Pause.*) 'To whomever it may concern.'

(*Elastic round letters, back under her skirts.*)
Still, this lot's good sorts. Poor. Very poor. Rollmops, cheese, and a bit of Jew-bread. That's poor. You can't get poorer than that!

(*Begins to clear away bits and pieces from drop leaf.*)
There's four of them. The master, the madam, the little master, and the little madam. The little madam's older than the little master! (*In one breath*) Effin' and blindin' and up and down these stairs and always with answers and his socks about his ankles and a tide-mark where his face is washed and his neck isn't and his friends yelling and his mother

always chasing and his father saying nothing or not much more than nothing – a right little master! I remember when he was born his grandmother took one look at him and said, 'He's either going to be a great man or a murderer!' Well on the way to being a murderer, I should think. Or murdered!

I nearly murdered him once. He come at my hat. Wanted it off. He stood over these railings here (*enacts scene*) as I was coming up the stairs, and he snatched! I got lots of needles in it so it didn't come away, but cor! did I jump and scream! 'My hat, my hat, my hat, no one's got the right to take my hat . . .' And I do believe my being upset made him upset, and my crying made him cry. 'You wear it all the time,' he tell me. 'We never see your head!' Well, what does anybody want to see my head for? That's not a head anybody would want to see, is it? Besides, I tell him. If I want to keep my head to myself, that's my right! That's *my* head, my head to do what I like with. Cover it, uncover it, smother it, cut it, perm it, dye it – what I like with it!

(*She's upset herself in the remembering. Needs to recover.*)
I'm bald under this hat. Got no hair worth speaking of. What'd he wanna go and upset me like that for?

(*Returns to packing away bundle.*)
He upsets everyone sooner or later. But they all love him! That's the funny part of it! They all love him but no one can control him. 'Cept his sister. She controls him. He listens to her. Very clever girl she is. Wears a school uniform from the Spitalfields Foundation School. Talks posh. Says (*blowing on each word*) 'Hwhen, hwhich and hwhether.' She's got all the world on her, that one. He listens to her. She's noble. She's noble but he's bonkers! (*Rolls a newspaper into a funnel.*) I once come early and he was still in bed and he'd made a tent out of this big feather cushion they sleep under – no blankets like us, but a big cushion, a deck they called it – and he was inside with a piece of rolled newspaper sticking out of the top, like a chimney, and he was speaking through it. 'This is the BBC Home Service. The Man in Black! Toot de toot, toot! Tonight's ghost story will be . . .' And then he'd tell this story to send shivers up you.

(*Rising*) The BBC Home Service! The Man in Black! (*Little dance.*) Toot de toot, toot!

(*She moves sadly to the pail on the stove.*)

Gawn! Bloody all dried up! Have to fill it again.

(*Takes hold of handle.*)

Oh! Cor bloody blimey that's bleedin' hot, if you'll forgive the French. Cor! (*Nurses hand.*) That hurt. As if I didn't have enough.

(*Takes a cloth and tries again. Fills pail with water, replaces it on stove. Regards hand. She's close to tears.*)

That'll bring a blister up, that'll bring a sodding blister up. Oh dear!

(*Sits. Mind wanders. Eyes glaze over. Dozes. Then – starts awake!*)

Hurrah! Hurrah! (*Pause.*) What did I say that for? What was I thinking of? (*Pause.*) Everyone's got a hurrah in them, Annie Wobbler. Even you used to say hurrah about something or other. But what?

(*Music: 'Ah, Sweet Mystery of Life.*)

Hurrah! Hurrah! Doesn't even sound like my voice. Sack o'coal! Sack o'coal. Hurrah! Hurrah!

(*Faint, sad echoes of a lost past.*

Hold. Then with glazed eyes she slowly rises, walks down stairs, turns her back to the audience, secretively, as though doing something in private. *)

The set slowly changes. She's unhooking her entire costume which – she throws off and away, sweeps her hat off her head, revealing – a strong young woman who is –

Part Two

ANNA

ANNA. *She is in black underwear, suspender belt and black stockings. Also black boots.*

She moves forward into new setting, takes a dress from off a full-length Victorian mirror, dances with it to the lilt of 'Ah, Sweet Mystery of Life'. Stops. Hangs it on hook on wall. Stands triumphantly before mirror as music ends.

* In the London production at the end of ANNIE, the actress walked slowly down the stairs to the front of the set. Between the railings, where a bar was missing, sat a bowl which looked as though it contained cat's milk. It contained oil with which the actress washed off her make-up using the tea cloths to wipe herself dry.

ANNA

What is there about you?

(*She's full of fun, over-brimming with energy, the world's before her.
But disturbing her sense of the future is a fear of what she might be
leaving behind, that she may not be what she feels she can be. She talks
to the image in the tall mirror when she's elsewhere in the room. In the
room there is also a Victorian dressing table on which is a typewriter, a
box of cosmetics, a small mirror (and other props which will be needed
in next scene). And a leather stool. Student digs. The place is London,
the dialect Yorkshire – or anywhere north of Birmingham and south of
Carlisle. The time is now.*)

It can't be your degree in French because he's got one in classics. It
must be your breasts.

(*She pulls down straps, saucily, and ambles with sedate dignity back
and forth.*)

'She walks in beauty, like the night . . .' (*Stops.*) And it would need
to be night.

(*She places mirror in a more comfortable position.*)

What is there about you? That trunk surely doesn't belong on those
legs. I think I'd better go back to the shop and get them to sort this lot
out, there's been a terrible mix-up here somewhere.

(*Attempts a Marilyn Monroe pose before mirror.*)

What *do* you think you're doing, Anna? And in black! My God!
You're so corny. If he's going to want you, it'll have to be for your
mind, the power of your intellect. (*Beat.*) Perhaps I'd better stick to
black underwear. No! You *have* got intellect. A first-class honours
degree in French, translations to and from! (*Ripping sheet out of
typewriter*) Offenbach!

(*Recited to her image in mirror*)

'Ne suis-je donc rien?
Que la tempête de passions s'apaise vers toi!
L'homme n'est plus; renais poète!
Je t'aime, Hoffmann. Appartiens-moi.'
But what does it mean?

Now stop that, Anna. This tedious English habit of boasting
ignorance. Three chaste and Cambridge years of slog – you know very
well what it means. (*Pause. Still regarding herself*) And take those
absurd boots off.

(*Grabs stool, sits to take off boots, translating meanwhile.*)

'Ne suis-je donc rien?'

Am I nothing?

'Que la tempête de passions s'apaise vers toi!'

Look how passion's tempests

Assuage around you . . .

'Assuage *around*'? Bloody hell, Anna! (*Thinking*) 'S'apaise vers toi!'

Ah! 'Deflate' around you.

Am I nothing?

How the tempestuous passions deflate around you . . .

Oh, good grief, Anna. Balloons and bladders deflate, not passions!

Be free! Free! Re-create the poem.

'And am I nothing? Look! Tempests and passions

Blaze around you.

The man is no more! Take hold, poet,

I love you! Belong to me!'

(*Her boots are off.*)

That's better. Great stuff! They don't talk like that today. (*To the mirror*) As the fat actor once said, 'You've got brains and black underwear? Flaunt them!'

(*Now she tries an assortment of high-heeled shoes, regarding herself in the mirror and chatting meanwhile.*)

Why *don't* the English like cleverness? We produce enough. 'Long live the simple man! Raw instinct! Salt of the earth! Knowledge destroys innocence!' Well, there was nothing charming about *my* innocence, I can tell you. Perpetual bewilderment! Non-stop ignorance! Didn't know if I was coming or going. Even when I was coming! Right, I said, must put a stop to all this. Goodbye, innocence, you've had your time. Innocence is for the innocent, and those who shall remain innocent when that time is done shall be called stupid, and the wrath of the Lord shall be upon them. Get thee with knowledge or thou wilt be got with child and an office job.

(*At this point she stands to regard herself in the mirror. Will this pair of shoes match?*)

So here I am. Educated!

(*Strutting as though at a cocktail party, shaking hands, nodding, bowing.*) And I shall not go naked into the literary cocktail parties, nor the political salons, nor the intimate dinners of erudite dons and heavyweight novelists, for I am armed with a set of cultural references which sparkle like a tiara of diamonds and announce to one and all who I am and the stuff of which I am made.

(*Coquettishly accepts an imaginary light to an imaginary cigarette from an imaginary, tall, dark stranger.*)

Thank you!

(*Catches herself in the mirror. Deflates.*)

But who are *you*! I've never seen *you* here before. Do you always go shopping like that? (*Pause.*) What is there about you? It can't be your body because it's kind of – odd! It can't be your black suspenders because he hasn't seen them yet. (*Pause.*) It must be an alchemy of the right mistakes which, against all the odds, combines to produce what they call *je ne sais quoi*! (*Beat.*) And neither does anybody else. (*Trying on a new pair*) On the other hand maybe the English think scholarship should conduct itself modestly. Unlike black underwear! Maybe they can't bear whorish scholars who parade like over-fleshed tarts in the corridors of academe. Ah! Perhaps that's what there is about you – you're not a scholar at all, you're an over-fleshed tart!

Yes, you bloody are a scholar! First-class honours degree in French! Against all the cultural odds. (*Calling out*) You hear that, mother, you old domesday book you? Your daughter's got a degree in froggy-talk! Tell that to Aunty Maud and all the others in *Coronation Street*! I've got brains and black underwear and I'm not ashamed! I–am–not–ashamed! (*Referring to her shoes*) Yes! These!

(*She sits before her dressing table and begins laying out her make-up.*)

The trouble is *he's* also clever. Difficult. *He* can be modest about his cleverness but *I* will have to hide *mine*, I can see. Why *don't* men like their women to be clever? They like them to be clever but not cleverer than them. Still, I don't suppose anybody enjoys anybody being cleverer than them. It's so undemocratic. (*Pause.*) Where's my black liner? What did I do with my black liner? Who has nicked my bloody black liner? What's the good of having black suspenders against my lily-white thighs if I've got no black liner for my lily-white eyes? (*Looking in mirror*) What lily-white eyes? How can I lengthen my saucers, darken my mystery, deepen my *Weltschmerz*? You mean melancholy, don't you, then say melancholy instead of all this foreign gibberish. You're English and living in England and we prefer straight plain honest Jane talk and calling a spade a spade and besides no one

knows what it means and where's my fucking eye-liner? (*Finds it.*) Ah!
Nearly had to call it off.

> (*Now all her bits and pieces are assembled ready for the long ritual.*
> *She begins, after a while.*)

What *is* there about you? I mean *that* is a face? The peak and epitome
of feminine beauty? Look at that nose. Grafted on at the last minute
from a mythological Greek. Clytemnostril! And that mouth! It's so
full of teeth it's bitten my lips away! Look at those teeth. Well, there
isn't anything else to look at, is there? And that chin! What chin? I
don't see a chin. (*To her image in long mirror*) Do you see a chin? I see
a neck, I see a face, but it's all one to me. And those eyes! Eternally
praying! I mean nothing, but nothing is right, is it? And yet (*drawing
herself up in profile*) there is a kind of haphazard beauty there. A kind of
accidental splendour. A kind of gargoylian loveliness. (*Beat.*) At least
nothing that a little bit of black liner can't put right.

> (*Continues to make up. We are witnessing an amazing trans-*
> *formation.*)

He says he can't bear women who make up. (*Beat.*) Tough shit!
(*Beat.*) Anna, you're coarse. *And* perverse. If he'd've said he loved
made-up women you'd've gone plain, wouldn't you! (*Quoting him*) 'I
mean, I don't object to the quantity you've got on *now*, but in excess
of that . . .' (*Beat.*) I wasn't wearing any fucking make-up! Anna,
Anna, Anna! Old women can't wear short skirts, nor can educated
ones cling to their cosy gutters.

> (*She concentrates on her making-up which is compelling watching.*
> *After a while –*)

Silenced yourself, haven't you? Think what you're going to do to him
then! (*Pause.*) I know, what about, what about listing the things you
don't like about him. That way he'll be a pleasant surprise.

He talks loudly. As though he's more interested to impress the
strangers nearby rather than the stunning woman before him, and
that I find mightily offensive as well as embarrassing. (*Pause.*) He
constructs his sentences like a bad Victorian Gothic novel.

(*Quoting him*) 'Yes! I have! I have read the entire *Divina Commedia*
of Dante, and what is more, though it becomes me not to say it, but
what I say is that only the *faint*-hearted are modest and God forbid I
should be quoted among *their* number, what is more I've read it in
Italian! Not, I might add, if I must be truthful – and I must for I'd be

loath to have you think me a fibster or dissembler, not that *all* its subtleties and nuances made themselves known to me, still! No small achievement, notwithstanding, for one so very English and reared to believe that all art the other side of the Channel was high falutin' codswallop!'

Well, more or less. And those long sentences! I find myself holding my breath and unable to put the next spoonful of crème brûlée into my mouth which stays open and ugly and makes people stare at me and Jesus Christ he's got me constructing them now!

He eats too quickly. *And* noisily. *And* insensitively. And he *insists* on everything! 'Might I suggest the little-known *poussin à la grecque* which I *insist* you try and which I guarantee will do things undreamt of to your taste-buds, the sensitivity of which will, hereafter, be offended by anything coarse. One *poussin à la grecque*, waiter, which the young lady would like with creamed spinach and sauté potatoes – trust me!' *C'était dégueulasse!* The Greeks don't bother with fucking *poussins!* Restaurants like that *cater* for the gullible like *him*.

And he's so *nice* about everybody. I told him: 'You're unbearable! You like everyone!' 'My goodness and fiddle dee dee,' he says, 'and what's wrong with that, pray?' He actually did say 'pray'. 'It's not that you like everyone,' I told him. 'It's what that implies.' 'Oh, and would it be too much to request of you an explanation of what it is that's implied?' (*She begins to talk like a Victorian Gothic novel.*) 'Yes,' I retorted, my nostrils flaring, my bosom heaving, and my heart pounding for the fray, 'if you like people it means that you don't envy them enough to dislike them, and what right have you to be so confident that nothing arouses your envy?' (*Beat.*) 'There's nothing in *me* you envy, damnit! That's terrible! That's insulting! It's so damn arrogant of you!' I could *see* he understood nothing! (*Beat.*) Nothing! (*Beat.*) Nothing!

And I'm convinced he quotes from books he's never read or don't exist.

And he dances like a broomstick.

And he doesn't like Barbra Streisand.

And, Jesus Christ, he doesn't make me laugh! What *am* I going on this date for?

(*Aware of herself now fully made up, and ravishing. With mounting triumph –*)

Because he's your first date since becoming a BA first-class honours and your cultural references shine like diamonds and you've broken the stranglehold of those century-old genes of crass ineptitude and supplication and you've unknown muscles to flex and a lot of intimidating to make up for and he's just the size and texture your teeth need sharpening upon! (*Grabs dress and holds it to herself before mirror.*) Upon which your teeth need sharpening! (*Puts it on.*) Upon which your teeth need! (*Beat.*) Upon which!

(*Stands tall before the mirror. She is stunning.*)

What *is* there about you?

(*Music: 'Ah, Sweet Mystery of Life'. Fade to half-light.*)

She unhitches dress beneath which is another, to become –

Part Three

ANNABELLA WHARTON I

ANNABELLA WHARTON, *aged forty-one, a novelist, in her new flat. She is dressed with intellectual as opposed to chic elegance. Beneath Anna's wig is revealed a severe bun.*

She is preparing for something. She folds the mirror to become a tapestry, an object she places somewhere, as a stand-in for someone. Who? What is about to happen? A VOICE OVER,* *echoing as though she's imagining it, is heard asking a question.*

VOICE OVER: (*A woman's, hard, brittle*) Miss Wharton, this is your fourth novel and, unlike the others, it's a phenomenal success. Instalments in the *Sunday Times*, translated into fourteen languages, the film rights sold for a quarter of a million dollars, the subject of controversy in the heavyweight literary journals. Annabella Wharton, what does it feel like being Annabella Wharton today?

(*She seems to be deciding how to answer it, which persona to adopt. Is she rehearsing for an interview?*)

ANNABELLA: Oh well, oh, well – er – to be honest . . .

(*Blackout.*)

* Both VOICE OVERS should be recorded by the actress.

Part Three

ANNABELLA WHARTON I

VOICE OVER: Miss Wharton, this is your fourth novel and, unlike the others, it's a phenomenal success. Instalments in *The Sunday Times*, translated into fourteen languages, the film rights sold for a quarter of a million dollars, the subject of controversy in the heavyweight literary journals. Annabella Wharton, what does it feel like being Annabella Wharton today?

ANNABELLA: Oh well, oh, well – er – to be honest . . . *

> (*After hesitation she decides on her persona: modest, self-effacing, bewildered. She puts half-glasses on her nose. Too high. Pushes them down.*)

. . . not much different, I'm afraid. (*Not bad. That's a voice that will amuse them.*) You'll still find me going up the road to buy fish and chips for my dinner some nights. (*And an attitude they'll warm to.*) Not much of a cook. Never was. Not that I don't like good food. As Dr Johnson says: 'He who doesn't mind his belly will hardly mind anything else!' But other people's good food. The kitchen confuses me, see. Never know what to reach for first. I mean you watch me fry an egg and you'd laugh. Burn the butter, crack the eggs before I've got the pan out, forget the toast, miss the plate. I mean, really, I find the material things of this world a bit double-dutch, so I can't quite understand the meaning of a quarter of a million dollars. It's a bit of a lark, if you ask me, isn't it? A lark! I mean – a quarter of a million!

Now where's that bottle of whisky? You will have a drink, won't you? 'Fraid whisky's all I've got, it's all I drink. Can't really bring myself to buy anything else. Not very polite of me, I know, ought to think of my friends and all those other visitors who come but, well, I get into the off-licence and I look at all that array of bottles and I think I can't choose from that lot, take me all day, and they're all synthetic, know what I mean? Concocted! Contrived! Experimental! Not like whisky. Whisky was always there, wasn't it?

> (*She finds bottle, and offers.*)

No? Oh well, I will. Need it. Cheers. (*Drinks.*) Besides, my

---

* If the play is performed without an interval, continue from this point, i.e. without the repetition.

accountant looks after things like money, and I tell him, 'It's your job, your decision, you work out what's best and tell me what to do and I'll do it.' So he's opened an account in Switzerland and it gathers interest, and every so often I go over there and fill my pockets and come home and pay my bills, and then I can attend to my writing. Fairyland I call it. Four times a year I hop on a plane and that's about the extent of my travelling. Cheers!

Hate travelling. The Brontës didn't need to travel and it suits me. I agree with Dr Johnson, you know, who, according to Boswell, agreed with the Lord Essex who advised the Earl of Rutland 'rather to go an hundred miles to speak with one wise man, than five miles to see a town'.

And I'm not sure I'd go five miles to speak to a wise man either.

(*Singing*) 'And as for fortune and as for fame . . .' Ha! I don't *feel* famous, I don't think I even comprehend the *nature* of fame. I mean I *know* I'm famous because people like you keep wanting to interview me and *tell* me I'm famous, but I don't actually know what I'm supposed to feel. Doesn't alter my conversation. I still can't talk at dinner parties or be witty or tell stories. I tell stories but I tell them badly. Forget the punch line or deliver it clumsily or get worked up in the middle instead of the end. And everybody else I know who writes seems to write better than I do, or about more important things than I do, so I really don't understand any of it. Here today and gone tomorrow. Will *you* come wanting to interview me if my next novel doesn't receive such favourable attention? Of course you won't! And I don't blame you. It's not really talent that's important, is it? I mean lots of writers are talented but not all that many sell their work for a quarter of a million dollars, so it's silly and nonsense and a bit of a lark.

(*Confidentially*) I'm what's called a mid-culture writer. I give people the *impression* I'm treating them intellectually without actually *calling* their intellect into play. People feel much more comfortable with that sort of work, which is why I've got all this attention. So there it is. That's how Annabella Wharton feels today, it's how Annabella Wharton felt yesterday, and, with God's grace and a bit of luck, that's how Annabella Wharton'll feel tomorrow.

VOICE OVER: Could you say what drives you to write?

ANNABELLA: Oh my goodness me, no. Oh good Lor', no. Drives me

99

to write? *Drives* me to write? Nothing *drives* me to write. I just potter around, you might say. Doodle. Start at the top of the page and work down. I'm not driven, I'm *used*! I start to create a character and suddenly – flip! There I am, dangled by him, or her, or it, puppet-like, made to do this then that then the other.

(*Reaches for her novel. Reads aloud, her tone serious now.*) 'It was the coldest day of the year. A desperate, cold, lonely day when lonely women commit cold and desperate acts they regret. Sara Newman would regret this day, it was certain, that.'

(*To herself*) 'It was certain, that'? (*Reflecting*) I didn't really need the word 'that'.

(*Back to sending up journalist*) There! When I put pen to paper to write those first three words, 'it was the', I didn't know the next word was going to be 'coldest'. It could've been 'hottest'. And if it had been 'hottest' then the rest of this prize-winning novel, *The Speechless Sick*, would've gone differently.

'It was the hottest day of the year. A defiant, rich and vibrant day when defiant women step out in control of their lives. Sarah Newman . . . etc. etc.'

And I didn't know her name would be Sara Newman, either. Where did *that* come from? You ask me! I couldn't tell you. And I didn't know she was going to be desperate and lonely either, poor thing. And so there I am, having to write about a lonely and desperate woman named Sara Newman. I didn't *want* to write about a lonely and desperate woman named Sara Newman. I'd actually decided that morning to start a novel about Mary Magdalene! Tossed about! Hooked! Dangled! Used! I'm not responsible for what I write, good Lor', no! Merely the medium through which they bring themselves to life. 'Not I! not I! but the wind that blows through me,' as D. H. Lawrence said, and many have agreed since.

VOICE OVER: Are you saying that no themes drive you, you've no wish to communicate a –

ANNABELLA: Don't say it! Terrible word! A message? God forbid! Messages? They'd have my guts for garters. On the other hand, on the other hand – if anybody needs to see something *in* my novels, fine! Very good! Glad to have been of service. That's their prerogative to interpret, take what they want, what they need. A good piece of literature is open to many interpretations, which is what I intend. As Dr Johnson, or someone, said: the smaller a work of art, the greater should be the co-efficient of expansion. God forbid I should mean *one* thing. Good Lor', no! I would like my work to be approached as one does a crossword puzzle. Clues! I give clues. That's what I write, a collection of clues. (*Confidentially*) Actually, to be honest, between thee and me, I just think I've been lucky to have struck a rather rich vein of contemporary stupidity!

VOICE OVER: Perhaps we ought to go back to beginnings and ask how and when did you begin writing?

ANNABELLA: Chinese poetry! Began with Chinese poetry! When I was fifteen and swotting for my mock exams I used the local reference library, one of those huge buildings harbouring statues of writers and thinkers from Cicero to Carlyle so beloved of those earnest Victorians, and among the books I discovered was one – *An Anthology of World Poetry*. (*Reaches from among books scattered over sofa.*) There was Latin poetry, yes, we'd done one or two of those; and Greek poetry, no, but not surprising, we'd heard the Greeks were once a great civilization; the Hebrews – the Hebrews? Oh yes, they'd written the Bible and parts of that counted as poetry. But then – Sanskrit? Japanese? Chinese? *Chinese?* The Chinese wrote poetry? I don't know why that should have struck me as improbable since I now know that everyone, everywhere, all the time has written poetry, but for some strange reason it came as a revelation or, to use the current jargon, a culture shock. And *what* poetry! So simple. So everyday, so delicate. I began at once to write Chinese poetry. By the time the evening was over I'd written half a dozen, by the time the week was through I'd filled half a school exercise book, and within a year I'd a whole volume ready for instant publication. I was launched! Or rather – struck! From that moment on I became a compulsive scribbler. Everything I saw, heard, experienced, went echoing round my head and became inexorably metamorphosed into literature: prose, a line of dialogue, Chinese poetry!
The leaves fall dead at my feet.
I walk home through them thinking of my tea.
I know it is autumn. In the front room there is a fire.
On the kitchen table are bangers and baked beans . . .
Easy, thoughtless. Began with Chinese poetry and now *no* one's safe from encounters with me.

VOICE OVER: Am I right in thinking you've been married once?

ANNABELLA: Good Lor', no! Never! Couldn't conceive of a man who'd want to share my scatty life. Unless he'd be prepared to cook for me and generally keep house. I did live with a man once, for three years. I don't really know whatever happened to him. After a few weeks I just realized that he wasn't there any more. He kind of evaporated away.

VOICE OVER: Do you have any children?

ANNABELLA: I don't think so.

VOICE OVER: You once said you write in your head. How do you remember it all?

ANNABELLA: Diary! I keep a diary. Every day. My obsession. I've got fifty volumes. Constantly dip into them.

VOICE OVER: Do you have any *bêtes noires*?

ANNABELLA: Not really. I think everything's a bit *bête noirey* once you get under the surface.

VOICE OVER: You have no fears?

ANNABELLA: O good Lor', yes. Everything frightens me. The morning, the doorbell, the telephone, interviewers, fish on the bone, the post, Dr Johnson . . .

VOICE OVER: Do you feel you have an endless flow of material?

ANNABELLA: . . . quarrelling cats, aeroplanes, ships, cars, bicycles, prams, politicians, mushrooms . . .

VOICE OVER: Do you feel you have an endless flow of material?

ANNABELLA: . . . heights, crowds, open spaces, closed spaces, three-point plugs, unboiled water, television news, ayatollahs . . .

VOICE OVER: But do you feel you have an endless flow of material?

ANNABELLA: (*Fiercely, the real Annabella*) I really do feel I've had enough of questions for today. Thank you.

(*The interview is over. Her eyes hold contempt. Then – she relaxes and a great change comes over her, of sadness, it seems, for the performance she has just now put up. She walks to a pile of her books on the cabinet, opens one to begin signing them. Has no will to. Reaches for a cigarette. The questions come at her again.*)

The second persona she adopts is tense, tough, a withering, witty intelligence.

ANNABELLA WHARTON II

VOICE OVER: (*A woman's. Eager, gushing*) Miss Wharton, this is your fourth novel and, unlike the others, it's a phenomenal success. Instalments in *The Sunday Times*, translated into fourteen languages, the film rights sold for a quarter of a million dollars, the subject of controversy in the heavyweight literary journals. Annabella Wharton, what does it feel like being Annabella Wharton today?

(*Long, long pause.*)

ANNABELLA: Fucking Empress of China! (*Pause.*) Well, you did ask.

VOICE OVER: Seriously now.

(*Long, long pause.*)

ANNABELLA: Fucking Empress of China! Nothing like it! High! I'm high all the time. To come to that dinner table throbbing with power from those detestable powerful people and have them begin to treat you with respect – nothing like it! It's cleansing, as though before – you were diseased, and now you're cured. The test is passed. Accepted! *You* know that *they* know that nothing can topple you now and that you can come and go and buy and match their extravagance-parading-as-generosity, and oh! there-is-nothing-like-it!

Does this shock you? This *is* the kind of thing you're looking for, isn't it?

Everything comes to you. Suddenly your past is unique. Suddenly your private life is fascinating. Suddenly you're photogenic, you're intelligent, you're an oracle, the look in your eye is feared. All that you've been saying for years that seemed presumptuous, misplaced, ill-conceived, and was greeted with bemused and mocking raised eyebrows, now appears wise, significant, valuable. 'Ah, this one knows what she's about and the world she's in!' Suddenly you're what the Irish call – a mensh!

But (*moving toward table/desk*) Most gratifying is that suddenly you've become a magnet! For offers of work, for interviews, for chat programmes, charity appeals, lectures, articles, comments on the latest political crisis or blunder, invitations to parties, a magnet for men! Oh for those men of superb intellect – and smutty appetites! And the awful thing is – it makes your lovely, neurotic, struggling

103

bohemian *former* self feel such a nonentity. A nothing! There she goes, weeping into the shadows, I don't need her, I don't know her. I glow with achievement. I blossom with arrival. I radiate and I'm ravishing and would change with no one.

(*She reaches for a hand mirror to check her make-up.*)

Empress of fucking China! No one!

VOICE OVER: I see. Could you say what drives you to write?

ANNABELLA: (*Into mirror*) Fame, Money and Power, I think.

VOICE OVER: No, seriously now.

ANNABELLA: Why do you imagine I'm *not* being serious? I write so that when I walk into a party there's a buzz, I'm looked at, regarded, wondered at. I write to be recognized in shops where I sign a cheque, on streets, at first nights. I write because artists who are successful are adored with a very special kind of passion I find my soul needs like a drug.

VOICE OVER: Are you saying that no theme drives you, you've no wish to communicate a –

ANNABELLA: – a message? Messages, said a Hollywood producer, are for Western Union! I tell stories. They're long, they're rich, they're true and those who have read them tell me they're spellbinding. Themes are for Ph.D.s and the Germans. As Dr Johnson has observed: 'Mankind have a great aversion to intellectual labour', and I for one have no wish to redirect such a powerful aversion since it wouldn't buy me the house of my dreams besides.

You're about to say you find that cynical. You probably think that everything I've said so far is cynical. Not true. I simply try to be honest. I'd like to present you (*briefly imitating the first Annabella*) a modest, humble personality, but that's not, I'm afraid, the way I feel. I can't cope with men's stupidities and endless cruelties, and so I'm contemptuous of all but a few very extraordinary people about whom I care passionately, from whom I can take anything and whose wisdom – and motives – I trust totally. My loyalties are reserved for them. Now criticize me, flaw me, despise me even, but you will never be able to write about me as a humbug.

How we doing? Is your tape working? The numbers of interviewers I've had who've put in their blank tapes and taken out their blank tapes.

VOICE OVER: Perhaps we ought to go back to beginnings and ask how and when did you begin writing?

ANNABELLA: Ah! How and when! Well, let's see. There were two stages, actually. First, dreadful poems and dreadful stories and then, well, it happened like this.

(*Begins to look in filing cabinet.*)

I had an uncle. Worked as a sub-editor on the *Daily Mirror*. He also wanted to write. Had some short stories printed in a London evening newspaper, couple of plays on radio, that sort of thing. But nothing more. I used to type my first poems on his typewriter.

(*Finds a file containing a letter.*)

And this uncle grew old and cynical like lots of people do and turned first to psychology and then to religion, and it was during his psychology period that, one day, I received a letter from him. (*Finds it.*) Momentous! He kept to himself most of the time, see, and when he *did* attend family dos his greatest pleasure was to adopt an aloof tone to any discussion that took place. So this letter, this letter was remarkable, remarkable for its absence of any cynicism whatsoever.

'Dear Annabella,' it said; he came from Wales.

(*She assumes a Welsh accent. 'Sings' the rhythm in the letter.*)

'Dear Annabella, I have something to reveal which I assure you will be beneficial to your future. Mornings usually will do. Yours, Uncle Dems. PS Keep this under your hat from the rest of the family.'

What could it be? It could be anything. Anything! A thousand pounds, perhaps, from insurance, which he wanted to give to me so's I could take a year off from work to write my first novel! Thrilling! It was a thrilling letter! A remarkable thrilling letter.

So I got up early next day, to get to him early so's I wouldn't be late for work – I was working in a vinegar factory at the time. My aunt let me in. He was still in bed.

'Oh no, I can't tell you! I've got cold feet. Forget it.'

'But Uncle Dems,' I say, 'I've got up specially early to come and see you. You might as well tell me now I'm here.'

'Oh, all right,' he says. 'I'll *tell* you why I asked you to come. I've been watching you,' he says. 'Over the years I've been watching you and I've come to the conclusion that I understand you. I understand you very well indeed. No one else in the family does, and no one else in the family would tell you what I'm going to tell you. But I *will* because I *do*. Now,' he says, 'you're not a very happy young woman. You're a good sort, intelligent but you're confused. And it's understandable. Perfectly! Your parents quarrelled and you loved them both and you've got a conflict raging inside you which is giving you complexes that'll destroy you unless you have them seen to.'

'Complexes, Uncle Dems? What complexes?'

'Delusions of grandeur!'

'Delusions of grandeur?!!'

'Delusions of grandeur! *You* want to be a writer! You'll *never* be a writer. Not in a hundred years, never! But there it is, this drive in you to compensate.

'And there's more! You're not a very imposing young woman are you?' In those days I *was* rather retiring and trying to hide myself so he was right, there. 'You're not a very imposing young woman and so you want to make up for it. Unhappy childhood, diminutive figure – classical! Perfectly understandably! Perfectly! I'm small and I wasn't happy either, and it affects people in different ways. Some want to be boxers, others want to be tycoons, some want to be Napoleon, and some want to be writers! And the world is full of unhappy people who are little people and there's only one Napoleon and one Rockefeller and onè Tolstoy –'

'*Was* Tolstoy small?' I asked him.

'Never in a hundred years will you publish a novel,' he said. 'I'll bet a hundred to one – your shilling to my five pounds,' he said, 'you'll never have a book published! And if you do, what then? You'll have to write another. And maybe, *maybe* that'll be published and your standard of living will go up and you'll have to write another and another and another – for fifty years assuming you'll live to seventy-five which God willing I hope you will and longer, for fifty years you'll be expected to turn out books. Non-stop! Because, you know,' he whispered it to me, 'you know that if you're silent for longer than two years out come those articles "Whatever happened to Annabella Wharton?" or "What and who were Annabella Wharton's enemies of promise?" I know,' he said. 'I've subbed them for the Sundays. And they're lethal. The world of literature', he warned me, 'is vituperative, snake-infested, full of academics and half-educated commentators trying to be Dr Johnson. Fifty years! And can you honestly tell me you've got all those books inside you? Can you? Psychiatry!' he counselled. 'There's the answer to your tears. Go and see a psychiatrist. He'll cure you of your delusions of grandeur. And that's what I have to tell you!'

No thousand pounds! But I was determined to win that fiver. And I did.

VOICE OVER: You once said you write in your head. How do you remember it all?

ANNABELLA: I keep a diary, don't I!

VOICE OVER: For posterity or insurance?

ANNABELLA: Oh, insurance! I listened well to Uncle Dems' warnings and they're all handwritten so's when the time comes they'll have a value as original manuscripts and copyright material for publication. As you can see, I trust no one. I'm building the most formidable castle I can against the vicissitudes of the outside world in general, and the certain betrayal of my public in particular.

VOICE OVER: Yes, I can see. I am right in thinking you've been married once?

ANNABELLA: Three times, actually. I've never mentioned the first two. They were nonentities and I felt rather ashamed to be caught ever having wanted such men. Now I feel strong and confident enough to own up to them.

VOICE OVER: Do you have any children?

ANNABELLA: At least four.

VOICE OVER: Do you have any *bêtes noires*?

ANNABELLA: Yes, people who sign petitions, attend conferences, and lecture on the meaning of art.

VOICE OVER: You have no fears?

ANNABELLA: Not now. None!

(*The interview is over. Her eyes hold contempt. Then – she relaxes and a great change comes over her, of sadness it seems, for the performance she had just now to put up. She's tired of play-acting. She's tired. Tired. She collects the pile of her books, brings them down to her desk to sign. Signs one. The light has faded. She moves to switch on standard lamp. The questions come at her again. Both voices. Insistent. She cannot hear them. Rushes to her cabinet for a sheet of paper, down to her typewriter, as though creativity will get rid of the questioning.*)

ANNABELLA WHARTON III

The voices of the first two interviewers echo out the first question again.

VOICES OVER: Miss Wharton, this is your fourth novel and . . . Miss Wharton, this is your fourth novel and . . . unlike the others it is a phenomenal success . . . unlike the others it is a phenomenal success . . . Annabella Wharton, what is it like being Annabella Wharton today?

    (*She can't write. Angrily snatches paper out of typewriter. Knocks her books to the floor.*)

ANNABELLA: (*Controlling herself*) 'Questioning', said Dr Johnson, 'is not the mode of conversation among gentlemen!' (*Gets on her knees to collect fallen books.*) 'It is assuming a superiority, and it is particularly wrong to question a man concerning himself. There may be', he said, 'parts of his former life which he may not wish to be made known to other persons, or even brought to his own recollections.' Dr Johnson! Not altogether true, I must admit. Sometimes I find myself with people so full of conversation and opinion and a retelling of their lives that I crave for one tiny question to be addressed to me. Eminently quotable, Dr Johnson, *and* contradictable.

    (*From here on* ANNABELLA *asks the questions herself, but still holding an imaginary exchange with the object standing in for the interviewer.*)

'What does it feel like being Annabella Wharton today?'

I'm not sure I can answer that. (*Tries hard.*) 'What does it feel like?' '*Feel* like?' Well, I'm gratified. Yes. I think I can safely say that. And I'm – relieved. Yes. I think I can safely say that. And I'm – well, well, to be honest – (*rises to take books back to cabinet*) I think it's a rather fatuous question. (*Beat.*) If you'll forgive me.

    (*She begins to unpin her hair.*)

'Could you say what drives you to write?'

(*She searches painfully, for the inexplicable. After a very long silence*) No.

Am I saying no theme drives me, no wish to communicate a message?

(*Thoughtfully*) People say they don't like messages. What do you think they mean? Do you think they'd rather the rose didn't tell them it was red? Or that people's eyes didn't speak? Or that there was never any writing on the wall? (*Pause.*) People are very odd, don't you think?

Or do you think they mean something else? 'Yes, we know all expressions convey a message but please, only those we *want* to hear, the old ones, you know, like "Death is the great leveller", or "Love is blind", or that one about, how does it go now? – "All men are equal".'

> (*She begins to unhook stockings and, with her back to the audience, unhooks black underwear so that she can in one go peel off underwear and dress turning to reveal a vulnerable middle-aged woman in bra and panties by end of next section.*)

One of the crassest utterances was uttered by a Hollywood film producer who said, 'Anyone wants to send a message they use Western Union.' While he himself spent millions on films communicating some of the most banal, shallowly felt, glibly expressed messages about life and death, crime and punishment, good and evil, love and hate, patriotism, nationalism, capitalism, liberty – *you* name it, *he* – misrepresented it.

(*Putting on her dressing gown*) Nevertheless, I try. I promise you I try to say nothing. Every morning I sit down at my desk I say, 'Annabella,' I say. 'Remember! Say nothing.' Every novel I write has on the front page of the manuscript: 'There is no significance to this story whatsoever. Any resemblance between this story and meaning is purely coincidental.'

'You say you write in your head. How do you remember it all?'

A notebook for notes. A diary for the truth. In the notebook I write: 'Today my son pissed on me.' In the diary I write: 'As one grows older one becomes more fascist! Fight it!'

'Perhaps we ought to go back to beginnings and ask how and when did you begin writing?'

(*Trying hard to remember*) There was a conversation I couldn't finish. Then! Was it then I began? (*Pause.*) Let's try again. There was a conversation I finished but wasn't satisfied with. Then? Was it then I began? I'm not sure that's true either. (*Thinks again.*) Was I in love with my English teacher? Inexpressible love? The shame of silence? (*Pause.*) I think I began writing when I wanted to affect others the way writers affected me. I think.

(*Fiercely*) You know, bad prose is like toffee in your mouth: the vowels fall back to front and the consonants prick like splinters, and your jaw seems to ache. (*Pause.*) That really didn't have anything to do with anything, did it?

How and when!

(*Rising*) Would you like some whisky? Or gin? Or vodka or brandy, perhaps? I've a full cupboard somewhere of so much, I've forgotten what I *have* got.

(*With sudden excitement*) It began with poetry. Why *is* it that a certain selection of words arranged in a certain way explodes in you and yet, change one word, one syllable and there's not even a damp spark?

(*Moving angrily to find poems in cabinet drawer. She finds sheets. Throws them around as she speaks.*)

I keep getting this urge, you see, to write poetry, it's a very strong urge and I become filled with a special kind of – kind of – how can it be described? An incorporeal expectation. A bit like being on heat. And out it comes, this poetry, this selection of words and images I *think* is poetry. And it's shit. And a pain. Such a pain. You've no idea the pain it is to begin with this heat, this fever, this sense that an astonishing assembly is about to take place and all that assembles is shit! Listen:

Well, world, you have kept faith with me,
    Kept faith with me.

Miraculous, aren't they? Thomas Hardy. Simple, but! a magic assembly. Now

– World world, you have kept faith with me . . .

Not quite the same is it?

Well world, you've kept your faith
    Kept your faith.

Not really.

Well, world with me your faith was kept
    Your faith was kept.

I don't think so.

Well, world, you have kept faith with me,
    Kept faith with me;
Upon the whole you have proved to be
    Much as you said you were.

(*Achingly*) To be a poet . . .

> (*From her cabinet she finds cream and cottonwool. It is time to remove the make-up from her face. She moves down to her desk and her mirror.*)

How many times married?

Once! To a man who was drawn by the heat but left . . .

Do I have any children?

A son. Who pisses over me.

Do I have any *bêtes noires*?

People who quote Dr Johnson.

You have no fears?

Of being afflicted with a sense of futility. Of violence and certitudes. Of failing my son. Of being disliked . . . mediocre. (*Pause.*) Somewhere within us *all* is a body waiting to give up, don't you think?

Do you feel you have an endless flow of material?

My father used to have a 78 record of a song called 'Ah, Sweet Mystery of Life', and he'd put it on and it would get stuck at the 'myst'. (*Gently sings it.*) 'Ah, sweet myst – sweet myst – sweet myst' – And then he'd push it and you'd get to 'life'. Well, I'm a bit like that. Stuck in the 'myst'.

> (*Singing*) 'Ah sweet myst – sweet myst – sweet myst – sweet myst – sweet myst – sweet myst – . . .'

> (*Music: 'Ah, Sweet Mystery of Life'. Lights slowly fade.*)